# PRAISE FOR
# THE EDUCATION OF WILL

"This powerful memoir twines the lives of an extraordinary dog and an extraordinary woman. Their courageous, compelling story will profoundly deepen your understanding of people and animals, fear and shame, love and listening."

—Sy Montgomery, author of *The Soul of an Octopus*

"This inspirational memoir is, above all, a book about redemption. McConnell faces her own history of trauma as she tries to understand and heal her fearful, reactive border collie Willie. Replete with McConnell's fascinating and often humorous insights about working with wonderful and sometimes wounded dogs, this is much more than a book about training dogs. *The Education of Will* engages in an intimate and challenging conversation with the reader about saving yourself, saving others, and allowing others to save you. It is original, powerful, heart-wrenching in its honesty—and filled with a comforting, gentle grace."

—Cat Warren, author of *What the Dog Knows*

"Patricia McConnell may be the finest popularizer of the science of animal behavior we have today, and for many dog owners—myself included—she's long been a wise and witty guiding light. With *The Education of Will*, her intensely personal and frankly brave memoir, she examines her own traumatic history with characteristic insight, honesty, and intellectual tenacity. The result is a fascinating portrait of the deepest of connections being forged between one woman and one dog—and just how high the stakes are for both. Patricia McConnell is a treasure, and we're very lucky indeed that she wrote this story."

—David Wroblewski, author of The Story of Edgar Sawtelle

"*The Education of Will* delves deep into the minds of people and dogs, and into the effects of trauma, showing that healing is possible. McConnell gives a voice to those who can't speak in words and provides hope for fearful animals everywhere."

—Temple Grandin, author of Animals Make Us Human<br>and Animals in Translation

"An unflinching look at trauma and how one woman grows beyond it—beside a wondrous, troubled spark of a dog who needs her help and helps her know herself. Wisdom earned in the hardest places, dog and human, carries with it a message of hope. *The Education of Will* is riveting from the first page to the last, and will reach many readers who long to put all kinds of burdens down."

—Susannah Charleson, author of Scent of the Missing<br>and The Possibility Dogs

"McConnell has written an inspiring and courageous book about the mysteries of the love between humans and dogs, and how that love can bring healing and forgiveness after trauma. Anyone who has ever loved a pet—especially a dog—will discover new and powerful insights into how that bond can lead to liberation, even from even our most hidden and crippling shames. *The Education of Will* brought me to tears and laughter, amazement and admiration. McConnell has dramatically advanced the growing body of literature that explores posttraumatic stress syndrome and how our life force—and that of our beloved dogs—leads us to truth-telling and a reconnection with ourselves and society."

—Nancy Venable Raine, author of After Silence

"In *The Education of Will*, Patricia McConnell writes with unflinching honesty, vulnerability, and warmth. She wraps her reader in the highs and lows of a life lived beautifully, through gut-wrenching traumas, hard-won victories, unexpected romances, and tear-jerking setbacks. Through it all, McConnell depicts the natural world (and, of course, dogs) with masterful reverence and passion. A tremendously winning memoir."

—Nickolas Butler, author of *Shotgun Lovesongs*,
*Beneath the Bonfire*, and *The Hearts of Men*

# PRAISE FOR
# THE OTHER END OF THE LEASH

"Patricia McConnell has written the *You Just Don't Understand* of the human-canine relationship. . . . This humorous, well-written book tells us what to do and what to avoid based on years of studying dogs and their primate owners."

—Frans de Waal, PhD, author of *Are We Smart Enough to
Know How Smart Animals Are?*

"A compassionate account of the reclamation of the author's life from abuse and shame. An uplifting story of hope about how both dogs and humans need 'a sense that they are not helpless victims.'"

—*Kirkus Reviews*

ALSO BY PATRICIA B. MCCONNELL

*The Other End of the Leash*
*For the Love of a Dog*
*The Puppy Primer*
*Love Has No Age Limit*
*Family Friendly Dog Training*
*The Cautious Canine*
*The Feisty Fido*
*Way to Go!*
*I'll Be Home Soon*
*Feeling Outnumbered?*
*Play Together, Stay Together*
*Tales of Two Species*

# THE
# EDUCATION
# OF WILL

Healing a Dog, Facing My Fears,
Reclaiming My Life

Patricia B. McConnell

**ATRIA** PAPERBACK

*New York · London · Toronto · Sydney · New Delhi*

ATRIA
PAPERBACK

An Imprint of Simon & Schuster, Inc.
1230 Avenue of the Americas
New York, NY 10020

First Atria Paperback edition February 2018

**ATRIA** PAPERBACK and colophon are trademarks of Simon & Schuster, Inc.

For information about special discounts for bulk purchases, please contact Simon & Schuster Special Sales at 1-866-506-1949 or business@simonandschuster.com.

The Simon & Schuster Speakers Bureau can bring authors to your live event. For more information or to book an event, contact the Simon & Schuster Speakers Bureau at 1-866-248-3049 or visit our website at www.simonspeakers.com.

Interior design by Kyoko Watanabe

Manufactured in the United States of America

10 9 8 7 6 5 4 3 2 1

The Library of Congress has cataloged the hardcover edition as follows:

Names: McConnell, Patricia B., author.
Title: The education of Will : a mutual memoir of a woman and her dog / Patricia B. McConnell.
Description: First Atria Books hardcover edition. | New York : Atria Books, 2017.
Identifiers: LCCN 2016029198 (print) | LCCN 2016054491 (ebook) |
    ISBN 9781501150159 (hardcover) | ISBN 9781501150173 (pbk.) |
    ISBN 9781501150203 (eBook)
Subjects: LCSH: Dogs—Behavior. | Dogs—Psychology. | Dog owners—Psychology. |
    Posttraumatic stress disorder—Patients. | McConnell, Patricia B. | Human-animal
    relationships.
Classification: LCC SF433.M337 2017 (print) | LCC SF433 (ebook) | DDC
    636.7/089689142—dc23
LC record available at https://lccn.loc.gov/2016029198

ISBN 978-1-5011-5015-9
ISBN 978-1-5011-5017-3 (pbk)
ISBN 978-1-5011-5020-3 (ebook)

To Jim

To Jen

To Willie

There's a crack in everything.
That's how the light gets in.

—*Leonard Cohen, "Anthem"*

# Author's Note

I started this book for myself, but I finished it for someone else. I don't know who that person might be, but if *The Education of Will* helps just one person as much as the book *After Silence* helped me, then it will be worth the five years it took for me to write it.

Like all memoirs, this is not an autobiography. Rather, it relates a slice of my life that I hope both informs and inspires the reader about the universal themes of trauma and forgiveness, fear and love. I have done my absolute best to portray the events in the book with as much accuracy as I can manage, although I did compress and simplify Willie's story of injury and recovery in a way that, I hope, prevents readers from getting lost in the details.

I have changed certain names and identifying characteristics. I have also modified the details of my clients and their dogs. In a few cases I combined their stories, but everything I write about them happened during the twenty-plus years in which I did behavioral consultations.

*The Education of Will* is my story—indeed, it is part of an effort to change my life story from one that worked against me to one that allows me to be closer to who I want to be. My deepest wish is that it helps others in the way that other books have helped me. However, I am not a psychologist or therapist, and nothing I write should be taken as professional advice to a reader who would be best served by consulting with someone in the appropriate profession. I hope also that this book will help readers understand that dogs, too, can be traumatized and need compassionate understanding as much as people do.

# THE EDUCATION OF WILL

# PROLOGUE

I was found early one morning in the desert outside the stable where I worked weekends. I had been lying on the cold, grainy sand for hours, listening to the high-pitched *who-whooo?* of burrowing owls and the metallic scurry of lizards. It was August 1966, and I had driven there at one in the morning in my family's powder-blue Mustang. I'd parked and walked around to the back of the stable, the black sky pinpointed with stars and a sliver of moon. Once behind the adobe buildings that held the sweet-smelling leather of saddles and bridles, I pulled my pink T-shirt partway up and unzipped my linen shorts. I lay down on the sand as if curling up in bed, the left side of my face to the ground. It was cold. I shivered a lot. Somewhere, far away, a pack of coyotes yip-yowled to the sky.

As I lay there, I remembered watching myself prepare to leave the house a half hour earlier, as if I were a disembodied ghost hovering over my body. I felt a kind of passive curiosity about this other creature who dressed as quietly as possible, crept into the kitchen, and picked up the keys to the car. Although I remembered nothing about driving to the stable, I could hear the horses shifting their feet in the sand as I walked behind the

1

buildings. After I lay down, I heard a quiet squeal after a thump of hooves landed on something thick and heavy, a squabble between two mares.

Once I positioned myself, it felt like days rather than hours until the sky began to lighten. My cheek began to hurt from the gravel underneath it, but I willed myself to stay still. All I could see was blackness, but I could smell the tangy scent of the creosote bushes and the ephemeral odor of newly cut hay. The owls hooted. The coyotes yipped. The hours dragged on as I lay in place, unable to move.

Morning finally arrived, and the sky lightened to the mauve of a desert sunrise. It was Karl who found me: Karl, the handsome Marlboro Man who was the lead wrangler at the stable and my first teenage crush. I heard the crunch of his boots becoming louder and louder. He bent down, and I turned toward him. His face had a look of disgust that broke my heart.

"Oh, Jesus, Trisha," he said. "What the hell?"

· · · · ·

I don't remember how I got home. I have no memory of the transition between stable and house, as though stage managers had rearranged the furniture between Act One and Act Two, out of sight of the audience.

My parents stood in the doorway, stunned and white-faced, asking me what happened.

"I'm not really sure," I said. "I went into the kitchen in the middle of the night to get some water, and a man grabbed me from behind. He put a damp rag over my mouth, and I passed out. He must have dragged me to the car, driven me to the stable. The next thing I knew, I woke up in the desert."

"Did he . . . ?" stammered my father.

"Oh, no," I said. "Nothing like that."

They didn't ask how I knew that, since supposedly I'd been unconscious. They didn't ask why a stranger had used our car to drive me to the stable, or why he had then left on foot. They did call the police, who arrived minutes later. The patrol officer had a gun strapped to his hip; the detective wore a rumpled suit.

I described the same scenario to them. The detective nodded and wrote notes. The officer sat quietly on our couch. Eventually, they asked if they could speak to my parents privately. I left the living room, walked numbly down the hall lined with family photos, and sat on my bed. I pulled Sniffles, a favorite stuffed animal, to my chest, and waited. I looked out the window at the saguaro cactus in the hills across the road. In just a few minutes, I heard my father's footsteps coming down the hall. He knocked lightly and opened the door.

"Trisha," he said. "The police are concerned that you aren't telling us exactly what happened. They could either ask you a lot more questions or drop the investigation if we agree not to pursue it. Would that be acceptable? To drop it?"

I nodded, unable to speak—just as I was unable to give voice to the reason I'd orchestrated the charade in the first place.

The police left, and my father called the editor of the local paper. A prominent businessman in Phoenix, he used his clout to keep the story under wraps. My mother warned me not to talk about it to anyone and worried how she would explain the police car to our neighbors.

After that, the house filled up with silence, like water rising in a fish tank. No one asked me what had really happened. No

one asked me if I was okay or what could have possibly motivated me to do such a thing.

We tiptoed around each other for days, talking about what
we'd eat for dinner or what was on television. Then the incident sank into the past, as if buried in wet sand after a flash
flood.

# CHAPTER ONE

The border collie puppy had eyes like fuzzy diamonds and fur so soft that my hands melted into it as if they had lost their bones. He was eight weeks old when I met him, sitting on the grass at his breeder's, with the sheep in the lambing shed bawling to their babies and the crickets buzzing in the woods behind the farmhouse. I didn't need another dog. I already had three, and I wasn't looking for a puppy.

I was busy. Busy seeing clients whose pets had serious behavior problems, teaching at the University of Wisconsin, cohosting a radio show, giving speeches on canine behavior, writing books, and running a dog-training business. I didn't need more to do.

But I had heard of a litter that was closely related to my once-in-a-lifetime dog, Cool Hand Luke. Luke had not only changed my life, he might have saved it, in a made-for-television moment when I came close to being horribly hurt and he could have died. I'd been pinned in a corner of a horse stall by a Scottish Black-face ewe who had just had a lamb and perceived me as a hungry wolf intent on killing her newborn. When she ducked her head and charged me the first time, I dodged to the right and laughed it off. Then she charged again and just missed me. Her head smashed into the barn wall so hard that a confetti of paint flakes fell from the ceiling. She charged once more and I retreated to a corner, looking around for a piece of wood, a bucket, anything I could use to protect myself.

We don't go through life aware of our own fragility until we have nothing but our own bodies to protect ourselves. No horns. No thick skin and fur. No bristles or claws. Useless little teeth. Put us up against an animal with a built-in security system and we come up short. I'd spent years as an applied animal behaviorist dealing with aggressive dogs. I was used to snarling canines of all kinds who would have bitten me if I'd made the wrong move. But I hadn't expected to be trapped in the corner of a barn by a crazed ewe.

Crystal the ewe charged again and grazed my thigh. She was known for her bad temper, but she was a sheep, not a two-thousand-pound bull or a muscled-up dog threatening to put me in the hospital. But my irritation began to morph into fear. I couldn't seem to get out of the corner and out of the pen. I was alone on the farm, and if I were badly injured, I wouldn't be missed for days.

That's when I heard it: *thwap!* Luke's paws hit the top of the four-foot stall as he scrambled over the pen like a military dog on maneuvers and hit the ground between Crystal and me. As she turned her attention to him, I scrambled toward the gate. Crystal tucked her head down so far that her chin was tucked under her chest, exposing only her two-inch-thick skull and curved horns. She went for Luke. He charged back, biting at her skull to keep her at bay while I made it out of the gate. After two more charges, Luke made his own escape. A thin stream of blood trickled from his mouth. Two of his front teeth had been broken off.

It is one thing to love a dog, to love him so much that sometimes you ache just talking about him. It is another thing altogether to know that he risked his life to save you from serious injury. But Luke was more than the star of this one dramatic moment; he was one of those old souls whose love of life leaves you glowing in its presence. I once wrote about Luke: "I imagine his death as if all the oxygen is sucked out of the air, and I am expected to live without it." Of course he died, and of course I didn't—but it took me years to stop grieving his untimely death from kidney failure when he was only twelve years old.

That was why the prospect of bringing home his nephew two years later was so seductive, despite having a house full of other dogs. All the dogs in Luke's line are famous for their noble dispositions; I had high hopes that this litter would have a pup with some of Luke's personality. Intellectually, I knew full well that every dog is unique, and dogs like Luke are hard to find. But still, how could I pass up the chance that one of the pups of the litter would replicate some of Luke's brilliance?

When I arrived to evaluate the litter, I pretended, mostly to myself, that I was making a careful and considered choice. The puppies tussled on the ground, interrupting their play only to leap after butterflies, sniff my jeans, or lick my face with velveteen tongues. I focused on the two male pups, since I had three females at home already. One male was a big, flashy boy with a wide white collar of fur, the other a bit plainer. I couldn't decide between them.

The breeder allowed to me to take them both home for a three-day trial period. It was a win/win—the pups would be exposed to a new environment at an important age, and I would see how they got along with my other dogs. After a few days, I could decide if one of them was right for me.

When I got home, the boys tumbled out of the crate as if out of a clown car. In turn, they met my three other dogs, each of whom performed a leading role at the farm. Tulip, the elderly Great Pyrenees whose radiance of white fur charmed everyone she met, was struggling with irritable bowel syndrome and a progressive neuromuscular disease. She'd been in the critical care unit at the local vet school three times that year. After each incident, she recovered and went back to being the farm's jokester, a cross between an oversize seal pup and a benevolent polar bear. For twelve years she had multitasked as the farm's protector and stand-up comedian. I felt I owed her anything I could do to keep her comfortable.

Pippy Tay, a fifteen-year-old border collie, had always been a paragon of health. For years, she was Watson to my Sherlock, assisting me in teasing out the reasons why so many of my clients' dogs were aggressive to members of their own species. Over the years I'd seen at least a hundred dogs standing stiff-legged and snarling while Pippy bowed and curtsied a safe distance away. Within minutes, the visiting dog would melt like ice cream in the sun, and soon they would be playing, while my clients' eyes filled with tears of happiness. But Pippy was losing her eyesight and hearing and had long since been retired. I was thrilled she had done so well for so long; I had never counted on her living to the ripe old age of fifteen. Like Tulip, she now needed a lot of care.

My third dog, Lassie, a twelve-year-old border collie, was the baby of the group. Vital and energetic, my go-to dog on sheep and still as playful as a puppy, Lassie nonetheless suffered from chronic bladder infections that belied her youthful looks. We spent untold hours with veterinarians trying to figure out what was wrong.

You might say that this was not an ideal time to get a puppy. You would be right. I calculated that I had been bringing my dogs to the vet 2.4 times a week for almost half a year. You know it's bad when you take the time to figure that out. With a decimal.

Did I really have the energy to raise a puppy? To be on guard at all times, to take the pup outside every ten minutes, and to gently remove the shoes, the remote control, or the pillow from its mouth? I had wanted a young dog for several years but had decided to wait until Pippy died. But even in old age, Pippy was thrilled when puppies visited, so I began to rethink my plan. Besides, I needed something healthy and joyful to make me laugh, to remind me that there was more to life than a slow spiral toward death.

Both pups settled into the farm quickly enough, following the tracks of chipmunks behind the house, playing with toys on the threadbare Oriental rug in the living room. But one of them followed me everywhere and seemed to care deeply about what I was doing and where I was going. His brother was better-looking but a bit more independent. Every time I gazed down at the plain one, he was looking up at me with soft, radiant eyes.

What is it about eyes that convey so much information but whose qualities seem beyond language? We have so few words to describe the depth of spirit and emotion conveyed by eyes that they all seem a bit trite. But it was his eyes that hooked me. I'd look down at this black-and-white fluff ball, and he'd gaze at me, his eyes looking deep into mine. Imploringly, as if always asking me a question. I didn't know what it was, but somehow it seemed imperative that I find the answer. I knew by the end of the first day that I couldn't let him go. I named him Will.

· · · · ·

That night, Will and I cuddled together on the living room floor, his little puppy body curled up on my stomach while the three girls encircled us. I stroked their bellies and scratched their ears and murmured to them that life was good, and no matter what happened next, love and determination would see us through.

# CHAPTER TWO

I live on a farm in southern Wisconsin, a twelve-acre parcel that I cherish and curse and can't imagine living without. The farm is tiny compared to the properties of my neighbors, who live on a hundred, two hundred, four hundred acres. I envy them their huge open fields and hour-long walks through the woods. But I fell in love with my land in 1982, the moment when I stepped out of a Realtor's car and stood on the hill overlooking the house.

I had already looked at the farmhouse—your basic black-and-white two-story structure replicated around the countryside like huge dice settled into the hills, with white siding, black window frames, and a porch sagging off the front of the house. The inside was a mess. There had been a fire upstairs, and the ceilings were black with smoke. The previous tenants had attempted to repair the damage done by the earlier renters—labeled "them hippies" by the neighbors—but the walls underneath the fake walnut paneling had so many cracks, it was unclear exactly what was holding up the house.

After the house tour, the Realtor drove me up a steep, rocky road to the field that overlooked the house and the valley in which it sat. As if in a dream, I walked out of the car and turned around 360 degrees to soak in the view of rolling hills covered by an oak-hickory forest. I trotted to the highest point of the field, where I could see the hills of Blue Mounds State Park. Huge white oak trees surrounded the field, their thick horizontal branches proclaiming access to the sun as they grew from acorns into guardians of the woods.

I looked down at the house nestled between the hills that cradled it like a cupped set of hands. I didn't care about the house—all I cared about was the view. As I stood at the highest point of the field, surrounded by hills and forest, I felt lighter, happier, as if something inside had softened in a way that made me stronger. I turned to the Realtor and blurted out, "This is it."

For years I had dreamed of living in the country in my own house, after decades in small apartments that smelled like cabbage or rented houses that could be sold out from under me at a moment's notice. But I never really believed it could happen until I stood in that field, turning around in circles, transfixed by the view. Over thirty years later, I still walk up the farm road and look at the surrounding hills, in awe that I live here. This is my farm, my land, my refuge.

I have lived on that farm by myself; with my ex-husband, Patrick; and now with my "third time's a charm" husband, Jim. I can't imagine being here without him. His voice is warm and kind and makes me happy to hear it. Before he retired, I used to call his office just to hear him speak his name on his answering machine. He likes my voice, too; that's how we met, from a voice message I left when I answered his personal ad in the newspaper, saying that I lived in the country with a flock of sheep. When he tried to call me back, the box number assigned to my message had expired. He told me later that he couldn't give up trying to find me because he loved my voice so much. He took out an ad in the paper that said in extra-large letters, "TRISHA WITH SHEEP, please call me."

I knew nothing of this until I opened up the local paper the next week. The bold letters of my name stared out at me like a private photograph that ends up on the Internet. I was mortified. There aren't a lot of people in my area named Trisha, and very few with sheep. It wasn't just my friends who could put those facts together; it was also the thousands of people who listened to the radio show I cohosted on Wisconsin Public Radio, *Calling All Pets*. I was fine with using personal ads, having been convinced by friends and colleagues that this was how one met people in the 2000s, but there is a reason they call them *personal* ads. Having a headline in the local paper that said "Trisha is looking for a man" was, as a good friend said, "like having your pants pulled down in public."

I wailed about the ad to my friends for a few days—how could a man be so oblivious as to put a woman's name in the paper?—and then life went on and I forgot about it. But it was in the paper again the next week. This time I called his number and asked if he would be so kind as cancel the ad, and gosh, I really wish he hadn't done it in the first place.

He apologized and said he'd put the ad in the paper because he couldn't bear not to meet me after hearing my voice. We talked for an hour. I liked his voice, too, so I agreed to meet him for coffee. He turned out to be about my height, with broad shoulders and arms as thick as my thigh. He had thick gray hair, the kind of strong, outdoorsy look that I've always loved, and a kind, open face.

He told me he lived in a condo, the perfect place because it gave him so much freedom. No snow to shovel. No lawn to mow. Lots of time to ride his bike and play soccer. "You'd be wise, then, to walk away right now," I said. "I have the biggest yard you've ever seen, and the chores never stop." He laughed.

I wasn't smitten. But something about him, something grounded and settled, gave me pause as I watched him walk to his car. It occurred to me that dating the men I'd fallen for at first glance hadn't worked out so well. Maybe I should see him again, just one more time? A week later, we had a drink together; dinner the week after; and eventually, we took the dogs down a wooded trail in an isolated county park on our first excursion alone.

The dogs ran ahead on the sun-dappled path while Jim and I talked about our careers. I told him about working with aggressive dogs. He told me about his job in a mental health institution with patients who at that time were called "the criminally insane." We compared notes about dealing with dangerous individuals—him with people, me with dogs—who could become violent if you made the wrong move. Currently, he explained, he worked at a state-run facility that confined and treated sexual predators.

Here's a tip for any man in the process of getting to know a woman you'd like to date: Keep the phrase "sexual predator" out of the conversation for as long as you can. Especially if it's your first time alone with her and you're in the middle of the woods.

Everything changed after I heard that phrase, as if a movie director had said "Cue the music," the kind of music you hear when a single woman walks down a dark stairway while the music tells you she's making a big mistake and you jump up and down on the couch saying, "Don't go down there, you idiot! Can't you hear the music?" The forest morphed from peaceful and serene to gloomy and threatening. I became hyperaware that it was just the two of us, that no one else was around, and that he was clearly as strong as an ox.

I wanted to go home and get away from this man whose life had something, anything, to do with sexual violence and predation. I walked faster, remembering something I simply had to do at home. Oh, look how the time has flown! It didn't matter that Jim had nothing to do with the perpetrators of sexual violence himself; he was in charge of human resources for the psychologists and caretakers who did. All that mattered to me was the phrase that linked "sexual" with "predation." Hearing it made me feel as raw as if I were covered with third-degree burns.

When we parted, he asked if he could call me again. I stayed quiet for a moment, loaded up the dogs, got into the driver's seat, and shut the door. I rolled down the window and told him that I would have to think about getting together again, a coward's version of "No, but I don't want to say that to your face." But something about him, an inner strength and kindness, stayed with me. A week later, I called him and confessed how distressed I had been in response to his occupation. His response was so understanding, so tender without being intrusive, that my fears began to recede. We talked for an hour. We met up again a few weeks later, and I began that beautiful slow-motion tango of falling in love.

· · · · ·

Jim and I are now partners on the farm and live surrounded by a multitude of wild animals, from crickets and mosquitoes to red-bellied woodpeckers and white-tailed deer. We love the country, but living here is not all sweetness and light. The hills, so scenic to live within, funnel water from spring rains and summer thunderstorms directly to the house and the barn. Jim and I battle with flowing water constantly, digging, channeling, damming it up relentlessly in an attempt to keep it from undermining the two structures. We win more battles than we lose, but the water wars will never be over. There are other challenges; there always are in the country. There are bramble bushes that grow everywhere except where you want them; brutally cold mornings that hurt your lungs while you feed the sheep; collapsing barns; and wild animals like raccoons and injured fawns that occasionally show up half-dead beside the farmhouse and demand that you drop your plans and deal with them.

It is also beautiful. As I write, I can see the hill that rises behind the house. It is bounded by a line of white pines planted by earlier owners, now towering fifty feet high. A chickadee is in the one of the trees, holding a sunflower seed between its feet, industriously pecking away at the shell. A squirrel leaps toward it from an adjacent tree, and the chickadee drops the seed and calls CHICK-A-DEE-DEE-DEE. Its music floats through the window and settles around me like a warm blanket on a January day.

# CHAPTER THREE

Will, who soon became Willie, lay curled up in the crate beside me as I drove him to his first vet appointment, a few days after I had returned his brother to the breeder. He kept his chin flat on the floor of the crate, his eyes looking into mine every time I glanced in his direction. The countryside was awash with the yellow of sunflowers and goldenrod and the green of head-high cornstalks. It was hot, so I parked in the shade on the side of the building, in a small lot bracketed by the drone of traffic and the sound of dogs barking.

As I lifted Willie from the car and the barking got louder, he panicked and flailed out of my arms with the strength of a dog ten times his size. He tumbled onto the ground and began streaking toward the road, moving as far away from the barking as he could get. An eight-week-old puppy is pretty fast, but I was able to catch up and grab him before he committed suicide on the highway. Hearts beating against each other's chests, I carried him back to the clinic, sat down on the cement steps, and held him as I tried to calm us both. It was unclear who was more frightened. After a few minutes it was time to move on, so I checked his collar and leash to ensure that they would stay attached. I checked them again. And again. I'd worked professionally with dogs for almost two decades by the time I got Willie, but the incident eroded my faith in my ability to keep a puppy safe.

When I set him down, Willie put his nose down in front of the clinic and began to sniff like an industrial vacuum cleaner, so hard that his nose was scraping against the concrete. I expected his nose to start lengthening like that of an animated creature in a Disney movie. My heart fell. I knew what this sniffing might mean. His uncle Luke would have quickly sniffed his way around the area and happily moved on, anticipating what was coming next. But there was no sense of curiosity in Willie's behavior; it was desperate and obsessive and foretold serious trouble as he got older. Early in my career I had seen a puppy named Yugo, a brindle-brown Labrador cross who entered my office as if his nose were attached to the carpet. He managed a weak wag when his olfactory investigations brought him close to me, but his head remained down and focused on the smells of other dogs. He returned in adolescence with a serious aggression problem toward other dogs. Since then, hundreds of dogs had entered my office and ignored me, slamming their noses to the ground, snorting their way around the room as they sucked up the scents of my four-legged clientele. It didn't matter if they were puppies, adolescents, or full-grown dogs, obsessive sniffing appeared to correlate with one thing: serious aggression toward other dogs.

As Willie snorted around, his nose pressed to the grass, I realized I had been holding my breath. I made myself take some deep breaths and waited for Willie to finish sniffing. He continued. I waited. The air forced in and out of his nose was so loud, it sounded like it was powered by an industrial bellows. Eventually, it was time to go inside. I called his name. No response; not even a flick of an ear. I crouched and held a treat within an inch of his nose. Nothing. Willie continued to suck up the dogs' scents like a dehydrated elephant at a water hole. After a few more attempts to lure him inside, I picked him up and carried him in.

One look at the receptionists and Willie melted into pudding. Eyes glowing, he licked faces and wagged his entire body, charming everyone. He thought nothing of his vaccination—he was too busy kissing the vet's face. Willie wiggled gleefully as the vet examined his mouth, and he squiggled and happy-faced his way throughout the entire exam. When we were done, the vet commented on what an adorable pup he was. I put him down on the floor, his puppy leash tangling around his oversize paws.

Willie and I smiled our way out into the lobby. Then, horror of horrors, we discovered a bichon frise puppy sitting on the linoleum like the disembodied tail of a rabbit. A bichon puppy is a tiny thing, as intimidating as a fluff of whipped cream. Unless you were Willie. All happiness gone, Willie's body went stiff, his mouth snapped shut, and he backed up as if he had seen a monster. I was looking at an adorable fuzzball of cuteness. He was looking at Godzilla. "Willie, Willie!" I said cheerfully, trying to jolly him up and show him there was nothing to be afraid of. He dived under a chair and began to growl. I took some more deep breaths, hauled him out, and put him in the car.

It might seem strange to worry about the behavior of an eight-week-old puppy, but animal behaviorists know that even young pups can act in ways that suggest serious problems later on in life. Did your pup chew up the remote control? Think nothing of it; that's as normal as a toddler who wants to put everything in her mouth. You expect it, deal with it, and it goes away. Did an eight-week-old pup go stiff and emit a menacing growl right out of a horror movie while standing over a piece of popcorn?

That's not typical and is predictive of serious trouble if not handled right away. Time to call a trainer or behaviorist—or maybe Stephen King with a scene suggestion.

The problem with Willie wasn't just *what* he was doing; it was *the age* at which he was doing it. His behavior replicated that of mature dogs whose extreme fear of other dogs had developed into teeth-bared, hard-eyed aggression. Adult behavior is rarely a good thing to see in a puppy, but it happens. "Puppies of the Corn," I call them: dogs who, like the glaze-eyed children in horror movies, are adorable one moment and terrifying another. Babies aren't supposed to act like aggressive grown-ups, and it is chilling when they do.

Once I was asked to evaluate a litter of seven-week-old Labrador puppies, and I was taken aback by their responses when I gently lay them down on their backs. Usually, puppies will squirm a bit and then settle down, perhaps mouthing your hands with bright eyes and cheerful faces. A few will go soft and still, eyes all liquid innocence. However, four of the puppies in this litter fought as though their lives depended on it, then went rigid while their eyes turned into cold, glittery marbles that stared straight into my own. If they'd had a gun, I think they would have used it. Two of them tried to leap up and bite my face, snarling as they did. Oh, my. I followed their progress and learned that three of them had been euthanized as young adults because they had bitten so many people.

With cases like that in mind, I called Willie's breeder when we got back home to ask if anything had happened in his past to explain his behavior. But nothing she knew of could explain Willie's reaction to other dogs. His parents had good dispositions, Willie had played well with his littermates, and she was aware of no traumatic incident related to the other dogs. Willie had seemed cautious when he first met my other dogs, but he'd quickly become comfortable around them. Lassie had even begun teaching him to play tug games with her. His behavior at the vet clinic was inexplicable. What could have happened to turn a squirming, happy-faced puppy into a terrified wreck in the presence of unfamiliar dogs?

· · · · ·

A few days after we returned from the clinic, a good friend brought over Comet, a mellow golden retriever who was famous for his benevolence toward puppies. Willie took one look at the dog placidly standing thirty yards away and began to growl. Then he began to bark like a police dog confronting a serial killer, his lips curled over his tiny puppy teeth, jagged white triangles in the sun. I asked him to back up, and I waited until he had stopped barking and growling, then I reinforced him for being quiet and a little bit calmer.

That afternoon I stood at the kitchen sink, worrying about Willie while I looked out the window, watching nuthatches flitting around the feeders full of sunflower seeds. Being trained to observe canine behavior is a mixed blessing, as experts can see trouble looming that others wouldn't notice. Some symptoms of behavioral problems, like those of many diseases, can be readily cured if addressed early on, before they become intractable. However, experience makes us especially wary about the slightest sign of trouble, which may not actually develop into a serious problem. Ignorance indeed can be bliss. Just because a child is slow to talk doesn't mean he will be diagnosed on the autism spectrum. Just because a puppy is terrified of other dogs doesn't mean he'll be aggressive.

But it might.

• • • • •

After dinner, I accidentally dropped a piece of broccoli that landed between Willie and Pippy, who leaned forward to slurp it up. In response, Willie charged at her like a junkyard dog at midnight. Eyes glaring, the corners of his mouth pushed forward in what is called an "offensive pucker," little Willie threw himself at Pip, challenging a dog six times his size. I'm not sure who was more surprised, Pippy or me. Reflexively—thank God for twenty-plus years of practice—I said, "WHAT are you doing!?" in a shocked voice. I stepped between him and Pip and moved Willie backward by walking toward him. I asked him to sit down. While he did, I fed Pip the food from the floor.

Then I gave Willie some treats while he was backed away, to teach him that good things happen if you are polite and patient but not if you are rude and pushy. Externally, I was calm and in control; I'd dealt with this type of dog behavior for so many years that I didn't need to stop and think about how to handle it. But knowing how to handle it was one thing; knowing that the puppy I'd already fallen in love with had serious aggression issues was another. A nine-week-old puppy who goes after an adult dog over a piece of broccoli is not behaving within the bell curve of normal development. Resource guarding is a common problem in dogs, but watching a baby puppy going after an adult dog over a vegetable is like watching a five-year-old boy threaten his mother with a butcher knife because she turned off the television.

• • • • •

That night I sat on the couch and worried about this bundle of behavioral problems that I had brought into the house. I turned to see Willie watching me, his face baby-soft and expectant, his body wagging from the shoulders back. I moved off the couch and lay down beside him. He nuzzled into me, the side of his head pressing against my neck. I inhaled the scent from the top of his head, as a girlfriend had told me she'd breathe in the smell of her son's hair, savor it, and yearn for it when they were apart.

Even as a tiny puppy, Willie wanted nothing more than to be with me, to cuddle against me with his face pressed against my neck or chest. Willie's love of people was as extreme as his fear of dogs outside of his own pack. He loved everyone on two legs and appeared to be overjoyed that the world contained an infinite number of us. When friends came over to meet Willie, he'd stop for a second as he watched them get out of their cars, seemingly stunned by the appearance of yet another person. He'd quickly glance at me as if in amazement—"Look! There's another one! I've found ANOTHER ONE!"—and then he'd charge forward, tail thumping, body soft and loose as he transported us into puppy rapture.

A lot of visitors came to the farm those first few weeks, and he charmed each of them. Willie was the perfect ambassador for his species, a public relations gold mine. He treated people as if each of us was the best present imaginable, wrapped up in a bow just for him. In the evening, he lay down beside me, snuggled deep against my heart, and licked my face with his skunky puppy breath. I forgot about his fears; I forgot about my own worries. My eyes closed as the light faded and the wood thrushes sang their fluted lullabies from the oaks behind the house.

# CHAPTER FOUR

The morning after Willie and I went to the vet clinic, Lassie came over and licked my hand, which dangled over the side of the bed. I stroked her face as sunrise lightened the room, and turned to cuddle next to Jim, who was snoring quietly beside me. We'd been together for six years by then, but he retained his condo in Madison and came out to the farm on weekends. Geriatric Pippy Tay was sound asleep but thumped her tail and opened her eyes when I said her name. In a few minutes, Pippy Tay arose from her dog bed, and I wrapped the pancakes of poop she'd passed in the night inside the tissues I'd learned to keep by the bed. Jim helped her get down the stairs, supporting her hindquarters and steadying her as she descended the steep, narrow passageway. I padded behind them to greet Tulip, at her post in the living room, and to let little Willie out of his crate.

I could smell it before I was halfway down the stairs, but the acrid stink of diarrhea did not prepare me for what I saw when I turned the corner into Willie's room. "Shit!" I said, with no conscious attempt at irony. It was everywhere, stinky brown frosting covering the inside of Willie's crate, Willie himself, and even several books on the bookshelf behind.

Little did I know that the pup who had stolen my heart had come with as much baggage as a starved, beaten dog from a puppy mill. Along with his terror of unfamiliar dogs, he had projectile diarrhea and spewed feces horizontally through the mesh of his crate or his exercise pen. No one knew why, even though I took him to my regular vet, to gastrointestinal specialists, to Chinese medicine vets and homeopathic vets. I read up on everything I could find about diet and healthy intestines. I cooked his meals myself, desperately trying to find a food that didn't cause an intestinal tsunami. Nothing seemed to help. I began almost every morning of my new life with Willie on my hands and knees, cleaning up liquid shit. As the days progressed, I got in the habit of hauling his crate into the bathtub to rinse it off. In spite of newspapers, protective plastic, and blankets, I spent hours on my hands and knees, scrubbing the floor to clean the cracks between the wooden planks.

And yet, once he was scrubbed up and clean again, he'd slide against me like a young kangaroo nuzzling into a pouch. He'd press his head against my neck and moan with happiness. I'd lie beside him, stroke his velvet belly, close my eyes, and forget about the poop and the vet visits and the medical bills stacking up on the counter.

· · · · ·

After a few weeks at the farm, Willie had learned a remarkable amount for his age. He could sit and lie down to the quietest cue and was learning to stay. Ridiculously responsive, he came every time I called, even if he was distracted—a behavior no one has a right to expect from a dog without months and months of training. He played tug games with Lassie every night; when she got tired, he'd play by himself if Jim and I were busy, flinging his bright red toy upward and catching it on its way down.

Now that he was settled into his new home, it was time to socialize Willie, to familiarize him with the scents, sights, and sounds of life off the farm. The country may hold its mysteries and adventures—chipmunks disappearing under bushes, crows scolding in the pines—but Willie needed to get into town, hear traffic, meet neighborhood children, and get accustomed to other dogs. I drove him to a neighborhood I knew well, a relatively quiet area with little traffic, a gaggle of young children playing a half block away, and no off-leash dogs to frighten him. Willie hopped out of the car happily enough but then stabbed his head down into the grass, sniffing the signposts of unfamiliar dogs as obsessively as he had at the vet clinic. Then a Buick appeared out of nowhere, woofers pounding out rap like Thor on a bender, and Willie's obsessive sniffing flipped into unmitigated terror.

He ran wild-eyed away from the noise, fighting the constraint of the leash and bucking like a lassoed mustang until I could get to him. I backed him away from the street and sat beside him, cooing to calm him. After he settled, we tried again to walk down the sidewalk. But our progress was not normal. Willie alternated between inhaling dog smells as if his life depended on it to all-out panic when he heard new noises, like a car or even the voices of children playing in the distance.

Within days, it became clear that Willie was as sensitive to sounds as any dog I had encountered in all my years of working with behavioral problems. When he was away from the country, even quiet noises terrified him. He was so afraid that I couldn't socialize him as I would a normal puppy; I would have to expose him to unfamiliar noises much more slowly than usual.

Even at the farm, there were plenty of noises for him to get used to. The peace of the country is an urban myth. Oh, it's blissfully quiet sometimes, but even if you can't see your closest neighbor, nearby tractors and four-wheelers often play backup to the song of a raucous flock of starlings. Living with nature isn't always a Bach sonata; sometimes it's a Rolling Stones concert.

Not long after our excursion into the city, someone started up a chain saw over the hill. One moment all we could hear were a few crows complaining in the woods; the next moment, full throttle, the entire farm seemed to be growling. Willie had been sleeping soundly on the rug but leaped to his feet, barks exploding out of his mouth like invisible bomb blasts. I dropped the glass I'd been holding and began to shake.

· · · · ·

I have never been brave. As a child, I spent my first day in kindergarten huddled in a corner, refusing to come out. My mother was asked not to bring me back. One of my earliest memories is not being able to sleep for weeks after being taken to a movie theater that had inadvertently switched a children's movie with an adult horror show. It featured massive robots that snatched people out of their homes and consumed them like monkeys eating grubs. My beleaguered mother pulled me and my sobbing five-year-old friends out of the theater as soon as she could, but I lay in bed for weeks afterward, staring at the window in my bedroom, listening to my sister Liza's metered breath as she slept, sure that at any moment the glass would shatter and I would be seized by a hand the size of a pickup truck, pulled through the window, and eaten alive.

Later, at the age of nineteen, I dreaded the days when my first husband, Doug, left town on business. I would pull the shades long before nightfall, terrified that I'd turn and see a face staring at me through the dark window glass. I'd sit on the couch with a book until I couldn't stay awake any longer. I didn't turn on the old black-and-white television because I didn't want to miss the sound of the doorknob turning if someone tried to break in. I couldn't shower, too vulnerable to be naked and helpless in the bathroom, so I'd wash my hair in the sink. After a while I couldn't avoid the image of someone creeping into the apartment while I was bent over the sink, so I let my hair get dirty until Doug came home.

I didn't think much about why I was so fearful. At the time it just seemed like another character flaw, like letting myself get too skinny or too fat, or being too shy to speak up when Doug's articulate, politically active friends came over for dinner. I had good reason to be frightened, but I got better at controlling—or at least hiding—my fears in my late twenties and early thirties. I still pulled the shades long before it got dark, but I was able to sleep in the bedroom instead of on the living room couch. I showered when alone, although I often kept the shower curtain partly open so I could see the bathroom door.

I told no one that several times a day I'd sense a man walking behind me with a baseball bat raised high behind him, like a major league star about to hit a home run. I knew that his next move was to smash the bat into my head, making it explode like a melon. Every time I sensed his presence, I sucked in my breath and jerked my head to look back. No one was ever there.

I hated going into dark rooms by myself. Sometimes I kept the lights on during the day. Other times I'd pace in front of a door leading into darkness and then work up the nerve to dash inside, like a mare running too fast at a jump that scares her.

Once I was able to flip the light switch, I'd look fearfully at the shower curtain or the closet door, afraid that someone was hiding behind it.

Things were easier for me years later when I had Luke, Willie's uncle. I don't know if he initiated going into dark places on his own or if I asked him to in the beginning, but I began to count on him to scout ahead of me, especially when I had to enter the barn at night. A classic red dairy barn, it was full of dark corners even with the lights on. Old implements and fencing materials were piled high in the corners, the perfect place for someone lying in wait, the natural habitat of serial killers. The kind with knives. When returning home after dark on bad days, I'd skip doing the sheep chores, too afraid to enter the building even with a flashlight, deeply ashamed of abandoning the flock until daylight.

Once I got Luke, everything changed. I'd open the old wooden door and back up a step, away from the darkness. Luke would run in, and after a few moments of silence, I'd know that nothing was there. No monsters under the bed or dangerous men hiding behind lumber and rolled-up wire fencing. I still didn't like being in the barn at night, and got out as soon as I could, but at least I could go inside and do what I needed to do.

But Willie wasn't Luke. He had his own monsters. Rather than helping me feel secure, he made my fear worse. Willie could scramble out of a dead sleep faster than your brain could process the word "startle." He'd be asleep one moment, perhaps cuddled against my shoulder in the evening, and the next instant he'd leap up into a stand, barking BARRR-RARR-BARR, his nails clawing my cheek.

Every time Willie leaped up to bark, often to a sound I couldn't even hear, I'd jerk up, too, and look around in a panic.

Heart pounding, sometimes nauseated with fear, I'd force myself to stop and take a breath. "Settle down, Willie," I'd say. *Calm down, Trisha*, I'd think. Forcing my body to go loose, taking slow breaths like I did with my clients' dogs, I did all I could to help both of us relax. But Willie would burst from silence into full-bore barking five or ten times in an evening. Even though I was soothed when we cuddled on the living room floor, his un-predictable explosions began to take a toll on me. I began to feel like I was living in a war zone, with IEDs scattered among the furniture in the living room. Dealing with my fears had always been a challenge, but now I was living with someone who was making them worse.

But then Willie would come over and lick my face. He'd drop a toy in my lap, his face radiating joy and love like a Hallmark commercial, and we'd play together like two kids in the backyard as the daylight faded and the moon rose behind the hill.

# CHAPTER FIVE

When I was five, someone asked me what I wanted to be when I grew up. I am told that I said, "I'm going to marry a rancher." One might argue that this foreshadowed my eventual attraction to strong, outdoorsy men, but more likely, it reflected my love for animals and my belief—reasonable at the time—that the only way to ensure being surrounded by animals was to marry someone who owned a lot of them. In Arizona in the early fifties, women had babies and made beds and tuna casseroles. Men had careers and made mortgage deals and shopping centers.

My father, a deeply conservative banker, believed for most of his life that women had no business interfering in a man's world. One night as I sat with my parents and my two older sisters at dinner, he carefully explained to us that women could never be promoted into an administration position at a bank because they couldn't be trusted to make good decisions.

"It's because of their monthlies," he stated while we sat around the new teak table paid for by his promotion at the bank. "Woman can be secretaries and teachers. Those are perfect jobs for them. Women are nurturing and supportive, and those positions don't require them to be assertive or to make difficult decisions."

Perhaps that is one of the reasons I arranged my collection of fifty-two stuffed animals—the big panda bear, the floppy, long-eared dog—in classroom-style seating every afternoon and stood before them with a miniature blackboard, teaching them to spell "cat" and "dog."

There is no doubt that my father loved his family and worried daily about providing for us. Often inaccessible to me when he was home and inside the house, my dad spent hours with me in his garden. He taught me to water his cherished roses ever so slowly, so the roots could absorb the moisture. I nodded in sympathy when he bemoaned that growing daffodils was impossible in the desert climate. He loved good books and good writing and took my sisters and me to the bookshelves in his den and selected just the right book for us at the right time. He told me once, reverentially, that books were like jewels in a treasure chest because you could open the cover and go anywhere in the world while sitting in a chair at home.

However, he encouraged us to read the thoughts of others, not to express our own. When my oldest sister, Wendy, was in her teens, she told him that she wanted to be a writer. He snorted: "What could you possibly have to say?" When my mother began leaving the house in the evenings to take a painting class, he would pace the driveway, a glass of Scotch and soda in his hand, his brow wrinkled, while she was gone. They usually fought after she returned, and eventually, even though she loved art and had real talent, she quit the class. My sisters and I were taught to stay quiet when Father came home from work. No talking to him, no loud laughter in another room, no running down the hallway. "Don't bother your father. He's had a hard day." Silence was important in my family.

I was shy and introverted. My best friend was a stuffed animal named Beauregard, an amorphous creamy-orange creature as big as I was. Beauregard went everywhere with me, slept with me, and listened to my deepest secrets. One day my father tossed Beauregard out of the car as we drove down a Colorado highway on a rare summer road trip, because I had thrown a fit at a rest stop: I wanted to drink out of a public drinking fountain that my mother deemed unsanitary. I cried, shrieked, and screamed, and continued to sob as we drove away. Normally a kind man, my father grabbed Beauregard in a fit of frustration and threw him out the window. My mother convinced him to turn around and retrieve Beauregard from where he was lying in the roadside grass.

By first grade, I had shifted my allegiance to real animals. Our terrier mix, Fudge, became my closest confidant, but my grand passion was horses. Just the sight of a horse made me happy. I begged my parents to let me ride the ponies at the fair when my legs were so short they stuck out straight from the saddle. My best friend and I played our own version of "horse," pointing our sneakers into hooves, tossing our cropped hair like manes, and prancing our way through recess, two awkward girls channeling powerful stallions. I drew horses constantly, specializing in the dished faces of Arabians and the muscled haunches of quarter horses. I collected equine figurines and spent a year teaching myself to make tiny leather bridles and saddles for them.

I was fascinated by other animals as well. I spent hours squatting in the dirt, watching ants as they traveled along tiny highways in the backyard. I taught Fudge to jump over a pole and to sit up and beg. I adopted a tarantula from science class and called her Lady Schick, an ironic title referring to her hairy legs and the new razor that had just come out for women only.

My mother, an avid animal lover, supported my efforts even

when it came to bringing home spiders. She saw that I loved animals as much as she did. She understood why I sat and watched ants, and she never criticized me for coming back inside covered in dirt. She appealed to my father's brother to pay for my riding camp in Montana after my father refused. Before I got my driver's license, she drove me back and forth to the stable every Saturday and Sunday, never complaining about getting up in the dark to do so.

But it was dogs she loved most; my sisters and I would tease her that she had more pictures of dogs on her wall than she did of us. Our family always had dogs, from Fudge the terrier mix to the Irish setters that Mother eventually bred and showed in conformation competitions around the country. Like many children with dogs, I'd lie on the floor and tell Fudge my childhood secrets, secure in the belief that she would understand me like no one else ever had.

Perhaps it is no surprise, then, that for twenty-five years I've used science, art, and empathy to help "problem dogs" have a voice; to listen to what they are trying to tell us and help them and their families be happy together. Willie was another one of those dogs, but this time he was mine. It seemed he had a lot to say.

# CHAPTER SIX

On a brisk midwestern day, puffy white clouds behind the woods, blaze-orange leaves polka-dotting the fading green, I was walking to the barn. Pip and Lassie led the way, furry dominoes loping gracefully through the grass. Three-month-old Willie stopped to sniff the greasy carcass of an earthworm. I was thinking about how much hay to give the sheep when a rabbit bolted out of the brush, streaking just a few feet in front of Willie. He took off in hot pursuit, his back legs overtaking his front ones like a cartoon character's as he tried to keep up.

My house and barn are too close to the road. I envy friends who measure their driveways in fractions of miles rather than yards. I've always lived in fear that I would lose a dog to the road, envisioning the pavement as a long, thin predator waiting to snatch up a member of my family and gobble it down. Although there's little traffic, the cars and trucks barrel past like freight trains, gravity pulling them down a steep hill on one side, a blind curve on the other. Much of the farm is fenced, but the front yard and the path to the barn are not. Rather than keep every dog on a leash until we get to a fenced area, I methodically teach our dogs never to go near the road; we never walk them anywhere near it, and they are taught to stop instantly and come when called. This wouldn't work, no matter how good the training, if I had a pack of bloodhounds bred to work independently, with their handler's job to follow as well as she can. But border collies are bred to listen even when running full tilt five hundred yards away. Although teaching them a "flying stop" takes time and effort, it is easily achievable if you make it a priority. City dwellers are appalled at the idea of a dog off leash; most country people can't imagine life any other way.

Once, when Lassie was younger, one of my ewes ran away from home. After a panicked search, I found her in a forest a few miles from the farm, with no way to capture her. I dashed home, terrified she'd disappear again, aware that only the magnetlike draw of other sheep would save her. Lassie helped me rush some of the flock up a ramp into my truck, all finesse thrown out the window, me yelling, "Get up, Lassie! Get 'em up!" With Lassie in the cab and the shocked sheep in the back, we drove up a steep, bumpy hill and let the group jump out of the truck beside the woods where the escapee stood trembling and ready to flee. As I had hoped, she left the woods and joined the safety of the flock. However, now I had six sheep standing in an open field several miles from home and no way to get them back—they could jump down out of the truck but not up into it. The only option was to have Lassie herd them down the hill a half mile to a neighbor's nearby barn, where they could stay overnight until I came up with a plan.

The next day, my friends and I figured Lassie and I could herd the sheep through unfenced fields and woods to a half mile from my farm. After that, we'd have to move the sheep down the county highway the rest of the way, with our cars in front of and behind the small flock. We picked a quiet time of day with little traffic, set our watches, and arranged a meeting time as if on a military maneuver. While I led the way, Lassie kept the sheep between her and me as we moved them out of the barn, up a hill toward a pasture, and down through a parcel of woods toward the road. By the time we got to the road, we'd walked less than a mile, yet I was already tired from the anxiety of losing the nervous sheep. As we descended a steep hill toward the highway, with my heart beating hard, I called to the drivers in the escort cars, who were waiting on either side of the trail as it joined the highway. Lassie eased the sheep onto the black asphalt between the escorts, and we proceeded like some midwestern cattle drive, car lights flashing.

Though it took only fifteen or twenty minutes on the pavement to finish the trip, it felt like forever. I hadn't anticipated what it would be like to see my dog on the road, walking as if naked in the jaws of the beast I had protected her from for so many years. By the time we made it back to the farm, I was a noodle. Next time a ewe goes AWOL, I'm building a loading ramp on-site. We may have dodged a bullet that day, but the road continues to lurk like a fat black snake.

· · · · ·

Willie was already ahead of the game in his training, staying atypically close to me and coming when called, but when the rabbit dashed out of the brush, he took off after it at a dead run—toward the road, only fifty yards away.

I reflexively shouted, "WILLIE!" In an instant he skidded to a stop, folded his body into a pretzel, and began to run back to me. I ran the other way to encourage him to chase me instead of the rabbit. When he caught up, I fell to the ground, singing out praise for a job well done: "Good boy! What a good boy!"

Willie's responsiveness was off the charts. I could whisper his name and he'd turn his head around to check in. If I said a quiet "Uh-uh," he'd instantly stop chewing on the table leg or jumping onto the counter. Someone once said that "our faults are the excesses of our virtues." How true that is, and how well Willie exemplified it. He'd flip around in an instant at a quiet word from me, but he'd startle two feet off the ground if I dropped something on the floor. He loved people passionately, but he reacted to unfamiliar dogs as if they were zombies approaching him with blood dripping from their mouths.

Something had sent Willie out into the world set on HIGH, like a blender with its last button pushed. Raising him was both wonderful and horrible. Underneath his craziness—his extreme reactions to unfamiliar dogs, his phobias about noises, his disastrous digestive system—I was sure there lived the dog we all want, brimming with love and loyalty, with a face that sparkles when you come home. But Willie desperately needed to feel safe and secure.

The thing was, so did I.

# CHAPTER SEVEN

When I was a young teenager, in 1964, I found a second home at a local stable, where my dreams of working with animals came true. Bonus: There were cowboys.

Tourists came to the stable and resort in Scottsdale, Arizona, for the warmth and the allure of cowboy hats and horses. "Easterners," we called them, envisioning Chicago as a western suburb of New York. Karl, the lead wrangler, tolerated me and the other girls who worked there, teasing us as we shoveled manure out of stalls and groomed the horses' shiny flanks. The girls and I talked about Karl as much as we did the horses. He had been in a Marlboro Man commercial, or at least that's what he told us. We never quite knew what role he played, but with his chiseled face and weathered tan, he could've been the Marlboro Man.

Bud was the second wrangler. Thin and spare like the dry-grass country he came from, he never said much. One day Bud was training two young horses to pull a wagon when one panicked and made a wild-eyed dash back to the barn. The scene was straight out of an old-fashioned Western—horses thundering down the lane with manes flowing, the wagon teetering on two wheels around the corners, reins flailing as Bud tried to regain control. He couldn't, and the wagon smashed into a cottonwood tree. It sounded like a bomb had gone off. When the dust settled, we could see that the horses weren't injured, but Bud's arm looked like hamburger. The other cowboys thought it was funny. Karl teased Bud about losing control of the horses; Bud grinned, shifted his hat, and bandaged his arm himself.

After a few years of slinging hay bales and saddling horses for the tourists, I was allowed to go out on trail rides as a second guide. I rode at the end of the line, keeping my eye on the greenhorns between me and Bud or Karl. Ever mindful of the potential for guests falling off their mounts, I'd trot up beside the blonde from Detroit with the turquoise necklace, or the redhead from Chicago wearing brand-new deerskin chaps, and chirp enthusiastically about sitting up straight in the saddle.

Karl and Bud were my heroes, the stars of my adolescent nighttime movies, in which I'd amaze and impress them with my horsemanship, my maturity, my own mane of tousled hair and smoldering beauty. No matter that my dark roots often showed beneath my Clairol-bleached hair, that I was skinny and flat-chested and couldn't have smoldered if you'd set me on fire. But I was coming into my own sexuality, spending my weekends with my legs wrapped around muscled horses and my mind increasingly distracted by Karl's tan forearms and Bud's blue eyes.

But the horses were what pulled me to the stable each weekend throughout high school. While other students attended football games or physics club meetings, I was at the stable every minute I could manage. I loved the horses' huge emotional eyes and arched necks, their velvet noses and broad, flat cheekbones. I loved the sounds they made—the syncopated rhythm of their hooves clopping on the packed dirt, the breathy snorts, the squeals of protest between fractious mares. I loved their smell, rich and pungent, deeply alive.

I loved riding them, too, and wanted to be brilliant at it. I wasn't. I was good, occasionally even very good, but I was too cautious, too frightened of being hurt to be the exceptional rider that I wanted to be. My innate lack of courage made me avoid risks. A group of us would race in an open area devoid of cactus and creosote bushes, with no adults around to stop us. As we entered the flats, we'd exchange glances like teenage boys in hot rods at a stoplight. Simultaneously, as if an invisible traffic light had turned green, we'd nestle into our saddles, lean forward, and let the horses run.

Each gait has a different feel. A horse with a smooth walk feels like a rocking chair. A trot is bouncy, though the trots of some horses are worse than others. You have to learn to loosen your hips and take some of the force there instead of in your backbone. A canter is smoother, and a gallop smoother still, although alarmingly fast for a novice. Still, there's nothing like being on a horse who switches from a casual gallop to an all-out, fast-as-you-can run. You may think you're already flying, shocked by the speed of the world streaming by and the power of the animal beneath you, but when your horse decides to run—*really* run—she extends her body forward and flattens out beneath you. The saddle, and your seat within it, lower as if a plane hit an air pocket and dropped fifty feet. It is one of the world's greatest feelings. I loved the rush of adrenaline, the sense of out-of-control freedom that came with it, and the power the horse's body gave mine. And yet I was always the first one to sit up and pull my horse back into a canter lest she step in a gopher hole or get carried away and refuse to stop.

My desire to impress Karl and Bud overrode my fears one

day, when they asked if I would ride the young stallion they had bought to run in some local quarter horse races. Money was in short supply, so they couldn't hire a real jockey. Would I—stick-skinny and light enough to be a jockey—ride this young stallion muscled up like a weight lifter on steroids, at least during training? I said yes.

I'd followed horse racing for years, cried bitter tears when Tim Tam broke his leg in the Belmont Stakes, and fantasized about being the first woman jockey to win the Kentucky Derby. This was my chance; my wildest dream had come true! We kept it quiet, an adolescent girl and two adult men, all knowing that what we were doing wouldn't fly with the stable owner or my father, who was so afraid of horses that he refused to let me own one, even when one was offered to me with free board and vet care. This would be our little secret.

A racing saddle is ridiculous. It is not designed to help you stay safely seated on a horse. Instead, it's all about the physics of forward motion and putting your weight exactly where your horse needs it to run his fastest. The stirrups are so high that you are essentially standing on the horse, with your knees bent at sharp angles to connect your butt with the horse's back. It feels like balancing on a tightrope while squatting as low as possible— and that's just when the horse is standing still.

For our first session, Karl hefted me up into the saddle, and the four of us walked out of the stable together: two cowboys with dreams of spare cash in their eyes, a young stallion the size of a tractor, and a skinny teenager too cowardly to say she was scared. We walked to an open area behind the stable. Karl led the horse by the halter while I tried to get used to the racing saddle.

After a few practice sessions during which I learned to be

even more frightened than before, I said, "I'm fine!" And yes, of course, we can go to the racetrack now and teach your big barely broke horse how to run out of a starting gate. On the way, Karl asked why I was so quiet.

I shrugged, my shoulders hunched between him and Bud in the cab. "I'm just excited."

After we unloaded the horse, Bud ground his Camel cigarette into the dirt and led us toward the enclosure. As we approached the gate, Karl said, "Get a good grip on the reins and then wrap your fingers in his mane. When he takes off, you'll have to hang on with your hands for the first few strides." I did as instructed, and soon Huge Horse and I were inserted into the gate, a claustrophia-inducing box with metal sides just inches from my knees. The horse shifted sideways, and I threw out my arm to save my leg from being squashed. I wanted out.

I forced myself to stay silent and concentrated on weaving my fingers, reins clasped in a death grip, into the horse's mane. Karl and Bud were talking, but I couldn't make out what they were saying. It was hot, and the sweat was beginning to drip down my forehead. I leaned forward and pushed my feet against the tiny, insanely high stirrups. Before I could take another breath, a sound like the end of the world blared out. The gate opened, and Huge Horse charged forward in terror. I lost my grip on his mane, and I was left two feet back from where I started, bouncing on his massive hindquarters but still hanging on to the reins as he thundered down the track.

What happened next is blurry—all I could see was a fuzz of fence posts and grandstands streaking by, as if I were looking out the window in a high-speed road race. I tried to pull myself back into the saddle, but that was akin to running on top of a moving train. Eventually, I realized that if I stayed still, I could ride it out, fists frozen on the reins, legs clasped around his hindquarters.

Huge Horse finally began to slow, and I realized that I wasn't going to die or be horrifically injured. But the horse wasn't the only one frightened by the unexpected blare of the bell and the crash of the starting gate opening. He had done what horses do when they are panicked: run. I had done what people do when they are terrified: pee my pants.

Karl and Bud met us at the far end of the track, and I slid off as the horse slowed to a walk, huffing with exertion. There was no way out of my humiliation: The dark stain on my jeans made clear what had happened.

"You okay?" Karl asked.

"Sure," I said. We loaded the stallion into the trailer and drove back to the stable in silence.

# CHAPTER EIGHT

That same year, my mother and I went to visit my uncle's family in Texas. My aunt, a refined Southerner from a well-to-do family, took us to their private country club for a ladies' lunch of club sandwiches under an umbrella overlooking the pool with iced tea in frosty pebbled glasses.

When the waiter came by, I said, "Nothing for me; I'm fine with something to drink." I explained to my aunt that I didn't eat lunch. Or breakfast. That I was on a diet and ate sparingly only at dinner. A few bites of meat. Ten peas. No potatoes.

"But you're so skinny!" she blurted out. She was right; I was five-eight and weighed less than 110 pounds. My goal was 105. Maybe I could get down to 100.

"You'd better be careful about not eating much," Aunt Pat said. "I just read an article about how dieting can get out of hand. It's called anorexia, and it can be dangerous."

My mother and I laughed. We knew nothing about anorexia, and in spite of the fact that my behavior and weight were classic signs of the disease, my aunt's concerns seemed overly dramatic. Mom always encouraged me to eat more, but you can't force food down an adolescent's throat. Besides, she understood how important it was to be attractive, which I desperately wanted to be. She wanted me to be, too.

My mom was gorgeous, a showstopping beauty who met my father while descending a staircase to see the son of her father's business partner, surrounded by a gaggle of his friends. One fellow took a look at her floating down the steps and fell to the ground, clutching his heart. It was one of her favorite stories.

I was the daughter whom she saw as best carrying on that tradition. My oldest sister, who wanted to be a writer, was designated the "sensitive one" (favorite color, assigned by my mother = blue). She was tall and blond, the kind of gangly teenager who grows into a beauty later in life but wears thick glasses and studiously hunches over a book during adolescence. The middle sister (green) was the "smart one." Active and gregarious, beloved by the teachers, she got high grades, participated in numerous committees, and acted in school plays. My color was red, and I was to be the "pretty one" who was taken shopping and enrolled in modeling school.

I was also the "easy one," at least the one Mom told me was "never any trouble." In reality, I probably caused as much trouble as any other kid, but my mother saw me as the "good girl" who could be counted on to stay quiet and not complain. Far less noble was my overwhelming need to keep the boat steady and avoid getting drenched when the family seas got stormy.

My parents fought, usually over money. The yelling came erratically, like summer thundershowers over the desert, the arguments punctuated by slammed doors and tight-lipped silences. My father sat in his chair every evening, nursing a weak Scotch and soda, brow wrinkled. Daddy was a worrier, deeply afraid of conflict or change. Once I was helping him change a lightbulb in the hallway ceiling when the doorbell rang unexpectedly;

he was on a stepladder, about to screw in the new bulb. "Oh, no!" he said. He descended from the ladder and began pacing in circles. "There is someone at the door!" he said, as if this were a crisis so serious that it was unclear how to handle it. With the condescension perfected by teenagers, I said, "Well, that IS terrible." I don't remember who it was; I just remember my father's flustered face and his panic. I wondered but never knew why this man—who ran a large business with what his colleagues saw as effortless grace—was so frightened.

Some of his worries were reasonable ones about money. The Depression had hit him hard as a child, and I suspect he had grown up believing that the world could fall out from underneath him at any time, as it had for many of his father's friends and colleagues. It didn't help that my mother loved to shop and spent money that he thought they could ill afford. On a bad night, my father would begin to yell, fueled by the Scotch and soda. After a fight my mother would retreat into herself, and the house would fill up for days or weeks with silence, the kind that makes the air so tight it feels hard to breathe.

When I turned fifteen, I bleached my hair blond. I wore miniskirts. I was given a negligée for Christmas. By my parents. Some quiet voice inside said, "This is not right," as I held it up out of the box, a sage green diaphanous thing with fake feathers on the hem.

In spite of our collective efforts, I saw myself as fat and unattractive, like many anorexics. I obsessively recorded what I ate each day and whether I had lost any weight. Every pound lost was a victory, every bite of uneaten food a triumph. I don't remember being hungry, although I did yearn for sugar. One week I tried bulimia—shaking sugar and cinnamon onto dozens of slices of buttered bread, putting them under the broiler until they crisped into the sweet, crunchy taste of badness. I ate the better part of an entire loaf of bread in one sitting. After a few unsuccessful attempts to purge it all into the toilet, I gave up and went back to eating almost nothing.

Mom would watch me eat dinner—ten peas, one ounce of meat, no potatoes—and shake her head. Sometimes we'd be joined at meals by my oldest sister, Wendy, now in her twenties, and her thirty-five-year-old boyfriend, Bruce. They were living in a guesthouse that had been built for my grandmother, who had long since passed away. Wendy had been ill; they had returned from out east so she could recover while living in the guesthouse for a few months. They arrived with Captain, a tongue-lolling black Labrador that Bruce and I began to take on walks together in the cactus-studded hills behind the house.

I volunteered to take the dog out by myself, to be free of my parents and the tension that permeated the house. I had begun sneaking cigarettes on these walks, which kept me skinny but allowed me to start eating more food. However, Bruce continued to walk with us, his long blond hair shining in the sun. We'd walk to a dirt road that wandered up the hills among the prickly pear cactus and creosote bushes. I didn't mind him coming, as he could be funny sometimes, but mostly, I wanted to be outside in the desert and out of the house.

One early summer day I needed to shop for a bathing suit. I was too young to drive myself, and for some reason—parents too busy?—Bruce was made driver and fashion consultant. After I tried on numerous suits and got thumbs-up or thumbs-down from Bruce, I settled on one and we drove back home, grinning like pirates in a B movie. I ran down the long hall into my bedroom and put on my new swimsuit while Bruce and my parents waited for me to model my new purchase. It was a bikini. An itsy-bitsy one.

The room went silent, except for the mockingbirds calling from the olive tree in the backyard. I spun around exuberantly, and then the circles slowed as my father said, his voice low and quiet, "You will return that bathing suit right now." Bruce winked at me when I walked back to my bedroom to take it off.

· · · · ·

He kissed me a few weeks later, suddenly turning to me on a walk through the desert and circling my head with his hands. Big and powerful, he radiated desire like some lothario out of a bodice-ripper. The only boys I had kissed up to then had been just that—boys—with awkward hands and noses in the wrong place, their breath smelling of potato chips. Bruce's kiss was a man's kiss, and it stopped my heart from beating for a moment. It also felt wrong, horribly wrong. I immediately pushed him away. But I couldn't push away the fact that, for one fleeting, involuntary moment, something in me had responded when he drew me to his chest. Maybe he realized that in spite of my telling him to leave me alone. Maybe he knew that, even though afterward I avoided him when I could, never again going on walks with him, avoiding eye contact. But the shadow of his presence never left me, always accompanied by the guilt I felt over my body's momentary reaction to him.

At the same time, my mother's lessons about being pretty became more complex. Yes, it was important to be beautiful, but there were dangers associated with it. She repeatedly told the story of how a workman, holding a carpet knife, had admired a recent photograph of me in their bedroom.

"He kept looking at you, holding that knife. It was awful."

"Oh, Mom," I'd say. "Don't be silly. He was holding a carpet knife because he was installing a new carpet! What's wrong with him saying something nice about the picture?"

Yet when she was gone, I'd look back at myself in the portrait and feel a chill. When I moved out of the house, I put the picture in the back of my new closet and didn't take it out for decades.

• • • • •

The first time Bruce crept into my bedroom, a few weeks after the kiss, I was sound asleep. I woke up in the dark to sense his face looming over mine. He had his huge right hand on my belly. The air conditioner kicked in as he began to smile. "Shhhhh," he said while slowly, almost reverentially, he pulled the covers down and my nightgown up.

"What are you doing? Get out of here!" I said.

"Don't say anything. You'll wake up your parents."

Their bedroom was close to mine. Trying to be quiet, I hissed at him again to go away. He said, "Do you really want to wake up everyone in the house?"

I stopped talking. The thought of causing more conflict in the family was paralyzing. The fights and the silences between my parents had intensified. Many of the fights that year were about Bruce, whom my mother disliked intensely. His bawdy jokes and Rabelaisian drinking appalled her, raised as she was to be a proper, stiff-upper-lipped Englishwoman. Things were especially tense because my oldest sister was ill, and we were all worried about her. Would she be okay? Would she recover? I loved her and admired her as only a little sister can, and I thought it would destroy her if she knew that her partner was being unfaithful. If I spoke out, then I would be causing her harm when she was already so vulnerable.

That first night, he ran his hands up and down my body while I lay motionless against the wall. Years earlier, a scorpion had fallen out of an air-conditioning vent above my bed, landed on my chest, and crawled up my neck onto my face. I thought if I moved, I'd make it sting me. I felt the same sense of paralysis when Bruce ran his hands up and down my belly, my baby breasts, my thighs; I was afraid to make a scene lest the entire family get stung.

He started coming into my room unpredictably; he'd appear one night, then not for the next two or three. I never knew when he would show up. He didn't rape me but instead seemed content with taking control of my body. He seemed to want only to look at my body and run his fat hands across it. He'd suck in his breath as he pulled down the bedspread, while I hissed to him to stop it, to go away. He always answered, "Go ahead, wake everyone up." I was forced to choose between tolerating his intrusions or breaking my sister's heart.

I would curl up against the wall when I heard his footsteps coming down the hallway. I lay frozen with revulsion as he touched me. I began to feel nauseated every night about the time he entered my bedroom, sick to my stomach as if I had eaten spoiled meat. I still sometimes feel physically ill when I hear about sexual violations. For years I would fight the urge to vomit when reading about the molestation of a young person.

The nights he didn't come were almost as bad as the ones he did. I stopped being able to sleep; the thought of him entering my bedroom when I was unconscious made me feel even more vulnerable. I began wearing more clothing to bed, but that just made it take longer for him to remove it.

It didn't go on for very long, because finally I rallied the strength to call his bluff. I said that if he didn't stop, I'd wake up the entire household. I'd tell my parents, I'd tell my sister, I'd yell and scream and blow the house down.

He never came back to my room at night, and eventually, my sister recovered from her illness. They moved to an apartment in another suburb. But even after they moved away, I would lie in bed for hours every night, ears straining, afraid to hear footsteps coming down the hall. Afraid I'd miss them if I didn't stay awake.

# CHAPTER NINE

One morning when Willie was five months old, Pippy didn't wake up when all the rest of us were buzzing around the room. I went over to her and stroked her shoulder. "Pip? Pippy, hon, wake up." Nothing. I spoke again, louder now, my throat closing when she didn't respond. I dreaded the day she would no longer be with us. Too fearful to stand up to the sheep, Pippy nonetheless was a perfect mother to her own pups and a nanny to the pups of others.

I thought of all that as I massaged her shoulder, hoping I hadn't lost her yet. She was partially blind, mostly deaf, and increasingly feeble, but she didn't seem to be suffering. Of course, how would I know? You can't ask dogs how they are feeling. They have no voice to tell you that their belly aches or that they're having a bad day. All I knew was that she still seemed to love naps in the sun, belly rubs in the evening, and most of all, the chicken and lamb we let her eat because . . . why not?

Finally, that morning, Pippy thumped her tail and lifted her head. I helped her out of her bed and guided her down the stairs. She rallied a bit, as she seemed to each day, ate her breakfast with vigor, and then lay back down for another nap.

As Pippy faltered, Willie improved. Gradually, his bouts of diarrhea became less frequent. I learned what he could eat and what he couldn't, and found a combination of supplements that helped him. Willie also made behavioral progress. A good friend volunteered to keep him while I was away on a book tour. We introduced him carefully to the resident dogs, and in no time at all Willie flourished in the company of other friendly border collies and four loving humans. This was a good start: He learned that at least some dogs outside of his own pack were not dangerous, and he romped and ran within a streaky blur of black and white.

When I returned home, we began a structured conditioning program to help him acclimate to unfamiliar dogs. I taught him to look at me when I said, "Watch," and then asked him to do it when he was sniffing the scent marks of other dogs. My first goal was to teach an "autowatch," in which Willie would automatically look at me when he saw another dog, instead of barking like a maniac. When he looked at me, he'd get a food treat or a play session with his favorite toy. If I did it right, he'd eventually associate the emotions he had when anticipating something good with seeing another dog. It's a technique that we trainers use often, but this time I needed it for my own dog.

Willie improved and became less reactive to the sight and smell of other dogs. He even began looking at dogs on walks as if he wanted to greet them, rather than freezing in a fixed stare with the tip of his tail wagging slowly and stiffly. (Slow wagging from a stiff-bodied dog is a behavior comparable to a lion's tail twitching as it stalks an antelope.) Now, sometimes, he'd wag from the shoulders back, his body loose, his mouth open, as if happy to see another dog. However, I didn't let him meet dogs I didn't know. That was far too risky, because I couldn't predict their behavior. We started walking parallel with dogs whom I trusted to be socially appropriate, first twenty feet apart, then ten, then five. Gradually, he became comfortable as they trotted side by side along the streets of Black Earth, our hometown.

These outings led to Willie making his first new friends: Ashby, a cheerful little springer bitch; and Sydney, an adolescent Australian sheepdog who loved to run with Willie in the high pasture overlooking the farmhouse. Willie began a bromance with Brody, a Cavalier King Charles spaniel who could come into the house without Willie objecting. They wrestle-played on the living room floor, charming us as we watched.

His circle of dog friends, however, was small. One day I asked a friend with a male black Lab to come over and help Willie in his conditioning program. Willie and I played the "watch" game outside until he looked comfortable, and then we let the boys loose in a fenced pen behind the farmhouse. Their greeting was polite, if a bit stiff, and once they seemed relaxed, we brought them into the house together.

Remember Jack Nicholson's face in *The Shining* when his character peers through a crack in a door, eyes burning with insane intensity, teeth bared as if ready to bite? That was Willie's expression once the two dogs entered the house. I simply cannot describe Willie's face at that moment without using the word "crazy." He looked so angry and evil that he seemed possessed. Yet this is the same dog whose face could be so soft and loving that sometimes I just had to stop what I was doing, bend my head forward, and rest it against his.

I told a friend about the dark side of Willie's behavior, and her eyes went blank as she turned her head ever so slightly to the side. She didn't believe me. Who could blame anyone for not believing that this exuberant, people-loving creature could panic if you put a bowl down too hard on the counter, or that he could look with murderous rage at another dog? Ninety-nine percent of the time, Willie was a glowing testament to why we love dogs. He was thrilled to meet visitors and bring them his toys. "A golden retriever in a tuxedo," I called him; he was loving and funny, radiating joy most of the time. Except when he didn't.

. . . . .

We all have a dark side. When I was in my teens and early twenties, I was the cheerful, funny one in school and at the office. A little shy, never one to join clubs or committees, I nonetheless could crack up my classmates or colleagues with a joke. No one knew that five or six times a day, while walking down the street, I would feel the presence of that faceless man who sneaked up behind me with a baseball bat, ready to kill me with one powerhouse blow to the head. I knew he wasn't really there, but the perception of his presence was so strong that I had to wheel around to check. I would try to ignore it, to continue walking purposefully forward, but the sensation was too intense. Eventually, I couldn't stop myself and would whirl around as fast as I could, trying to catch sight of him before he disappeared. And then it would happen an hour later while I was walking with a friend, and I would sneak a look behind me as she chattered on about her date the night before. I'd see nothing but sidewalk and lawn and trees, and I'd turn back and try to keep up with our conversation.

# CHAPTER TEN

By spring 2007, Willie was an adolescent. The red-winged blackbirds were back; their cries of CONK-A-REE! drifted through the trees as Willie and I walked up the hill for one of his first sheepherding lessons. The path was lined with stately oaks and upstart honeysuckle bushes. While we walked, a flock of turkeys flushed in a cacophony of gobbling, as if the forest floor itself had arisen. The snow was finally gone in the high pasture, although hard, dirty patches lay like moldering icebergs on the shady side of the barn.

At nine months of age, Willie was ready to begin learning to be a sheepdog. It's not the calendar that tells you when a border collie is ready; it's the dog. He needs to be mature enough to be able to outrun the sheep, but just as important, his heart and his head must be in the right place. Some dogs are keen to work sheep at six months, some not until they are much older. You can't decide for them, and you can't ask them, either—not verbally, anyway. The only way you can ask the question "Are you ready?" is to put them in with sheep. The answer is what happens next.

Youngsters who aren't ready will avoid the sheep by studiously sniffing the ground, or they will be distracted by butterflies. Then one day a switch gets flipped: You take them into a pen with sheep and their heads sink down, their eyes focus as if everything else in the world has fallen away, and there is nothing but the sheep. Seeing a young dog "turn on to sheep" will give you goose bumps. It's beautiful and riveting—the dog's intent focus draws you in like a black hole pulls in energy. And at nine months, Willie's switch had flipped.

However, his first efforts were less than ideal. Before he was allowed in with the flock, he barked at them across the fence. This was a sign of fear and not what you want to see in a young dog. After he stopped barking, he would dash back and forth along the fence line and then charge toward the flock, scattering the panicked sheep. This is a terrible habit for a dog to learn and, once started, is tough to break. Nervous dogs love to bully the sheep, to make them move by charging them, rather than quietly and confidently taking control. So I squelched this bad habit by not allowing him to come with me to do the barn chores; Willie had to stay in the house when I fed the flock.

Once Willie had matured into late adolescence, he had enough physical ability and emotional maturity to begin training, so I put him in with sheep for the first time at a good friend's farm. Peg had a small fenced area with enough room for the dog to work, but not so much space that we couldn't stop things before they got out of control. The word "control" should be used loosely when introducing dogs to sheep. The dog needs to learn to move on his own, to be free to find that magic zone where his actions allow him to manage the sheep without panicking them. Most handlers put young dogs in with sheep who are accustomed to dogs, then do all they can to stay between the sheep and the dog to protect the sheep if necessary. (Sometimes it is the dog that you have to protect—sheep don't watch the movies and aren't aware that they are supposed to be helpless victims.) It's like white-water kayaking, in which you study the route, prepare your equipment, and practice your skills; ultimately, you have to put your boat into the river and let the water catch you up and sweep you away.

Anything can happen when a young border collie is let loose with sheep for the first time. On rare occasions, a young dog takes one look at the sheep, runs around them in a perfect semi-circle, and quietly brings them to you, the flock neatly served up like a martini at a five-star restaurant. That's what happened the first time I introduced eleven-month-old Lassie to sheep. She had arrived at the farm the night before, scheduled to stay just a few days as a favor to her breeder. Having grown up in the suburbs, she had never seen sheep in her life. Out of curiosity, I let her loose in my smallest pasture, where she ran around to the other side of the flock, stopped exactly where she should, and carefully walked the sheep up to me as if she'd had months of training. I called the breeder and asked if I could keep her.

Willie was a more typical young dog. When the sheep began to move, he charged forward and chased them. He thought it was great fun, but chasing a flock of sheep like a group of tennis balls is not herding them, and running away from a dog isn't good for sheep. It took one more session to get him to stop chasing, and several more for him to get the courage to go between the sheep and the fence in order to peel them off and bring them to me.

Sheep are neither dumb nor defenseless. They learn fast that if they hug the fence, a young dog will have to push its way between their bodies and a hard, solid structure to get them off. Ewes weigh 100 to 180 pounds and have heads like hammers, while herding dogs are all of thirty or forty pounds. Aggressive sheep are perfectly capable of smashing a dog into a fence post and ending its career before it even starts. Good handlers carefully select the sheep for a dog's first lessons—not so aggressive that they'll attack the dog, but not so flighty that they'll attempt to sail over the fence like clumsy deer if the dog gets to chasing.

Essentially, sheep herding is about managing fear. Sheep are prey animals, and although they'll stand and fight if they have no choice, they prefer to move away from danger. They're also social creatures and understand fractions in the only way they need to: If there are a hundred sheep, their chance of being killed by a predator is only one in a hundred. If there are ten, it's one in ten. If there is only one of them . . . even they can do the math. Sheep want to be in a group, the larger the better, and they want to be able to move away from danger.

A good dog manages sheep by finding just the right distance and pace to move the sheep by intimidating but not frightening them. Too close or too fast and the sheep will either dash away in a panic or turn and fight. Too far away or too cautious and the sheep lose respect for the dog and ignore or attack it. This distance between dog and sheep—the sweet spot that allows your dog to take control of the sheep without overwhelming them—is called the "balance point," and it's the goal of all shepherds who value the welfare of their sheep. The right distance between dog and sheep varies—flighty sheep require dogs to work far away, while "heavy" ones, less responsive to a dog's presence, need a dog to work much closer. Sheep are only one of the variables; different dogs work the same sheep at different distances. Some dogs have more presence, more natural power, that somehow takes over the flock's psyche and moves it away without creating a panic. Less confident dogs need to get closer, sometimes weaving back and forth in an attempt to use movement to push the sheep, instead of the calm, steady confidence that defines a great sheepdog.

Starting a young dog on sheep is not for the faint of heart. You are balancing three sets of fears: the sheep's, your dog's, and your own. At some point, you just have to take off the leash and let the universe decide what happens next. That was part of why Willie and I were at Peg's. She had appropriate sheep and an appropriate enclosure, and she had a lot more experience than I did with starting young dogs. It had been almost fifteen years since I had introduced a young dog to sheep. Part of doing a good job is knowing when to interfere, which requires the reaction time of a soccer goalie. The other part is knowing when to stay out of the way. That's even harder.

Willie was clearly keen to work but frightened to get too close to the sheep. For several sessions, I had to gently take hold of his collar and ease him between the sheep and the fence to teach him that it was safe to push between them. Rather than walking up in the stalking posture of a hunting lion, as confident border collies do, Willie preferred to run back and forth behind the sheep, using movement to urge the sheep to me. He also liked to bust in on the sheep before circling to the back, a regressive return to the behavior he had tried at the fence when he was younger. He didn't bite or chase; instead, he just charged forward with his eyes sparkling and sent the sheep scrambling in all directions like balls breaking on a pool table.

Clearly, he enjoyed the game: *Eeee-ha! Look at 'em scramble!* So after a few freebies that all youngsters are allowed in order to keep them keen, I got between him and the sheep and walked toward him, pushing him back from the sheep and letting him circle the sheep again at a correct distance. Every sheepdog needs to learn that there are rules to the game, just like kids learn that hitting the pitcher with a bat is not playing baseball. But if you follow the rules, you get to keep working—something a good border collie wants more than all the treats in a pet store combined.

We began working together at home, and slowly, gradually, Willie gained confidence. He stopped busting in on the sheep and began to trust his ability to move the flock without dashing back and forth. He was incredibly easy to work, responsive and obedient and quick to stop when asked. Too much so, in some ways. After I'd trained with him at the farm for several months, one of the country's top trainers, Alasdair MacRae, watched Willie work at one of his clinics and said that his obedient nature was the flip side of his hesitation to put pressure on the sheep. My job was to encourage him to walk steadily and consistently, maintaining "contact" with the flock. "Don't worry too much about pace yet," Alasdair said. "Just keep him moving straight on and let him get comfortable with the feeling of putting some pressure on the sheep." That's what we did. Willie began to show me what it was like to face one's fears head-on, his head and tail in a stalking posture, his eyes focused, the sheep grudgingly trotting around the pasture day after day, the redstart warblers for whom the farm is named singing, Red red red red REDSTART! all around us.

# Chapter Eleven

When I was twenty-eight, my first marriage ended and I moved to Madison, Wisconsin. Two years later, I was flat broke and miserable. One Thursday I took a day off work to sit in a puddle of misery on the floor of my tiny lakeside apartment. Here I was, almost thirty, with no money and no hope for a future in my present job as an administrative assistant at a nonprofit that advocated for alcohol and other drug abuse agencies. I'd already been a volunteer worker at a stable, a salesgirl in a clothing boutique, a glorified secretary at a television studio, a checkout clerk, an unofficial Teacher Corps member, a statistical typist, a counselor for troubled adolescents, and for one ridiculous and dimly remembered night, a go-go girl hired to dance at a private party.

I wasn't crazy about my job at the nonprofit, but I did enjoy organizing our annual conference. During my last year there, I was also responsible for presenting a talk on the importance of including women in treatment plans for alcoholics. (At the time, "alcoholics" were always assumed to be male, and treatment plans assumed the clientele would be exclusively male. Women were more often given tranquilizers than diagnosed with alcoholism.) An hour before my presentation, with me nervous about the talk and already managing dozens of conference details, the director asked if I could fill in at a meeting and take notes.

Now? Really? Of course I said yes. I walked into a conference room with fifteen men sitting around a table. I sat down, and the director said his name and asked others to introduce themselves. That man to his left introduced himself, then turned to the next person to do the same.

My heart sped up as the participants introduced themselves around the table. Soon it would be my turn to speak. My hands began to shake, and it became increasingly difficult to write the names of the attendees. All my life I had been terrified of talking in front of people. My throat closed up and my mind went blank whenever people turned and looked at me expectantly. I even took up needlework in my twenties so that I could avoid eye contact when surrounded by my first husband's colleagues.

The introductions around the table were getting closer to me. I practiced in my head what I would say: "I'm Patricia McConnell, and I'm the administrative assistant."

I needn't have worried. The man to my right said his piece and then turned his head in my direction. As I was opening my mouth to say my name, the man to my left spoke over me. It hadn't occurred to him that I would introduce myself. As the recording secretary and the only woman in the group, I wasn't expected to have a voice. As I sat in stunned silence, my face hot with humiliation, the introductions continued around the table.

I would like to tell you that I began my career solely because of a deep-seated passion for animals. It's true that this was my primary motivation. But underneath my love of animals, I was motivated by something else. After years of feeling like I had no voice, I wanted to be the one with something to say, even though I was afraid to do so. Everyone needs a voice and needs to be listened to. Including dogs. Maybe I could give them that. Maybe I could give it to myself.

· · · · ·

I was thirty years old when I entered the University of Wisconsin–Madison as a freshman in 1978. I didn't go back to school expecting to work with aggressive dogs but focused on studying the behavior of all animals. I got a bachelor of science in zoology, then worked for two years with cotton-top tamarins, a squirrel-sized, terminally cute monkey with Einstein-like hair and a lust for mealworms. Soon after, I went to graduate school to continue learning about animal behavior.

My research in graduate school began with an undergraduate honors thesis, required for my zoology degree in my senior year. I needed a topic and an adviser and was referred to Professor Jeffrey Baylis as an expert in animal behavior. I wanted to study communication between people and animals and thought I might write about research on using visual symbols to communicate with dolphins.

"Not a lot of dolphins in Wisconsin," Baylis said dismissively. My heart fell; I thought I'd come up with a great idea. He went on, "Why don't you study a natural form of communication between species and look at the signals that shepherds give to their working dogs while they manage their flocks of sheep?" Baylis knew about this nuanced communication because he'd spent time in Montana, where vast flocks of sheep dot the countryside.

*What a stupid idea,* I thought as I drove home after our meeting. Where the hell was I going to find a sheepdog trainer in Wisconsin, the land of the dairy cow? I thought I'd have a better chance of finding dolphins swimming in Lake Michigan than people who managed a flock with working sheepdogs.

Sometimes it is wonderful to be wrong. By the next day, I had discovered that one of the country's top sheepdog trainers, Jack Knox, lived just an hour away from me. He had come from England a few years before and brought a century of sheepherding wisdom with him. I drove up to meet him and his dogs a few days later.

Jack introduced me to a couple of his dogs, then led me to a lush, expansive pasture with sheep grazing four or five hundred yards away. Jan, his petite all-black border collie, trotted by his side. The three of us stopped as a red-tailed hawk circled overhead, calling out in its hoarse, dinosaurian voice as it rode the currents. Jack whispered something, so quietly I didn't hear what, and Jan instantly streaked away to our left as if propelled by a force too strong to be contained in her tight little body. She ran in a huge half circle around to the back of the flock, shrinking into a tiny black dot as she got farther away. Once behind the sheep, she lowered her head and crept toward them like a cat stalking a mouse.

Slowly, carefully, she eased the flock to us, never letting up on the pressure but never pushing so hard that she scared the sheep into a panicked run. She lay down once the sheep were deposited at our feet, but she never wavered in her laserlike focus on one member of the flock. "She's watching the lead ewe," Jack explained. "A good dog evaluates the entire flock as she runs around them, turning her head to look at them every twenty yards or so. By the time she's behind them, she's figured out where they want to go once they start moving, and which one is the flock leader. That's part of the dog's job, to 'read the sheep,' because they do it much better than we do. Our job as handlers is to tell the dog where we want the sheep to go—sometimes into the barn for safety from coyotes, sometimes into a new pasture. In sheepdog competitions, the dog and handler work as a team to move the sheep through a complicated course."

Oh, my. What I had just seen left me smitten, gob-smacked, falling down the rabbit hole. The complex communication between sheep and dog and handler was riveting, and beyond anything I had dreamed of in my desire to study communication between two different species. As if that weren't enough, the setting was stunning. The dogs' contrasting colors popped out from the green background as if designed by a graphic artist. Watching the dogs work was like stepping inside a calendar of scenic Ireland, pages flipped to the month of May.

I couldn't get enough of seeing Jack work the older dogs and train the young ones, and often drove up to his farm to take notes on visual communication between dog and sheep and the acoustic communication from handler to dog. The verbal and whistle signals from the handlers to the dogs have to be clear and concise, because the dogs' eyes must be fixated on the sheep to maintain control. Even better, because one of "my species" was human, I could ask the handler the meaning of the signal or what he wanted the dog to do after he called or whistled.

I traveled to a sheepdog trial in Tucson, Arizona, where I recorded the whistle signals used by fourteen handlers to maneuver their dogs around the course; then I came home and measured every possible parameter I could manage. I sorted all the sonograms (think "pictures of sound") into categories: "Walk Up" and "Lie Down" to encourage or discourage forward movement, "Come Bye" and "Away to Me" to circle clockwise or counterclockwise around the flock.

Once I looked at the whistles as pictures, I saw that all the Walk Up whistles were similar—short, rapidly repeated notes. All of the Lie Down signals were similar, too, but looked like opposites of Walk Up—single notes, often long continuous ones that dropped down at the end. You could randomly pull out one of the whistles that changed a dog's movement (start versus stop) and immediately know what it told the dog to do.

It made sense that so many whistles sounded alike. Whistles are passed on from handler to handler, and they might have been examples of what biologists call "cultural transmission"—or behavior passed on through teaching and learning rather than through the genetic code. But if that was true, why did the directional signals vary so much? If signals were learned and used like words in a language, why were some shared by all the handlers and some not?

That question pulled me back to graduate school. I had loved my two years of working with cotton-top tamarins, but my heart remained with the dogs.

One day I was pondering why some whistles followed a pattern and others didn't while riding a sweet Arabian gelding through the woods. The wind came up, and my horse began to fuss at the strange smells, throwing up his head, trotting in jagged sideways steps instead of his usual smooth walk. "Whoaaaaa," I said, extending the word into a long continuous note. He stopped, and I saw what I had said as a picture in my mind, just like the pictures of the whistles that handlers use to slow down their dogs. Without thinking, I clicked to him to begin to move forward, using the same short repeated notes that handlers use to speed up their dogs.

I suspect that the clouds didn't part and the angels didn't actually sing, but the moment when I linked the sounds of sheepdog handlers and horseback riders was one that a scientist may be lucky enough to get once or twice in her life. Eureka! Immediately, I saw the pattern: short repeated notes to speed animals up, long continuous ones to soothe or to slow. The more I thought about it, the more examples I could recall of signals to domestic animals following the same pattern. "Pup pup pup," we call to encourage a young dog to us. "E-a-a-a-sy," we say to a frightened horse. But why? Is it because we humans tend to use sounds that reflect what we want, either because we're primates and make such sounds naturally—think of the "hoo hoo hoo" of an excited chimpanzee—or might we link certain sounds with an expected outcome because it's more effective?

That is the question I went back to graduate school to answer: Are certain types of sounds better than others at getting animals to speed up or slow down, or do we use similar sounds because of tradition? If the former is true, then people all over the world should use similar sounds to encourage their animals to move forward or stop moving, no matter what language they speak or what animal they are working with. Thus began three years of recording more than a hundred animal handlers, from as many fields as I could find, including people working with sheep, sled and protection dogs, and race, dressage, rodeo, and working cattle horses. I even managed to record a variety of handlers "talking" to cats, domestic fowl ("How do you call your chickens back to the roost?"), water buffalo, camels, and llamas. I was able to record handlers speaking in seventeen languages, including

Navajos speeding up their horses and Korean cat owners calling to their cats.

For my first fieldwork I traveled to Texas to record Spanish-speaking jockeys at a racetrack in Texas between Dallas and Fort Worth. In Dallas, I picked up my rental car and drove to the track to meet up with the trainer. I was curious to see the track: My images of racetracks were formed by watching the Triple Crown—the Kentucky Derby, the Preakness, and the Belmont, bustling with horses sparkling like massive animated jewels, stables nicer than most of the places I'd lived as a young adult, and walking paths lined with carefully tended roses and carnations.

But this track fit none of those images. I turned in on a dirt road and parked between crumbling wooden structures so decrepit that I expected them to collapse in front of me. I hefted a heavy reel-to-reel Uher tape recorder over my shoulder, hung my camera over the other, and began to look for the man who had agreed to meet with me. It was hot, quiet, and dusty. Not a bird was singing, but I could hear faint music coming from one of the stalls in a stable block. I walked toward it, told my heart to stop pounding against my chest, and poked my head into the darkness of an unlighted stall.

"Hello?" I squeaked. "I'm looking for Roger. Is he here?"

Three dimly lit figures leaped to their feet. Two disappeared behind some hay bales, grabbing unidentifiable objects that had been sitting in front of them. The remaining one stared back at me in shock; I'm not sure which of us was more frightened. I seemed to be walking into a dystopian movie scene in which life as I knew it had come to an end. Things weren't so good from his perspective, either. Here was a stranger with a tape recorder and a camera in what, I later learned, was a drug-infested den of iniquity that had been closed down by the racing authorities.

I managed to repeat my question. "Is Roger here?"

"No, not here," he said, and disappeared into the back of the stall.

I continued to wander around, never finding Roger, but another trainer took pity on me and did what he could to help me. "Trisha," he said after I explained why I was there, "you should not be here. There've been three murders here in the last few months. Very dangerous here."

Oh. I explained how far I had come and how important it was for me to record horse handlers who used a language other than English. "Well, then, come back tomorrow, when Marco is here. He's a good guy. He knows everybody, and he'll help you out."

Marco was as friendly and accommodating as described. He spent the day driving me to a variety of horse farms and training stables. He translated and explained, managed fractious horses, and enabled a treasure chest of recordings of Spanish speakers working with their horses. I ignored the fat, oblong packages of dried herbs he slid to the trainers when he arrived, and I graciously declined his offer of a joint the size of a cigar. I also declined his invitation to stop and watch the sunset over a nearby lake on our way home. "Really, Marco, you've been great, but I have to get back to analyze the recordings."

The time-honored conversation between a young, healthy male and an unwilling female continued until, finally, the man who'd understood that my interest was all about sound said, "But Trisha, please come to the lake with me. I will make you such beautiful noises."

· · · · ·

After Texas, I spent a summer in Montana recording Spanish, Basque, and Quechua-speaking sheepdog handlers and horseback riders on sprawling western sheep ranches. I can't say why, but I don't remember ever being frightened in Montana. Some of the time I was with family, but much of the time I was alone in isolated areas, surrounded by men who spoke foreign languages. I might have been nervous about getting good recordings, or managing the camper I pulled behind Black Bart, my beat-up pickup truck, but I never felt the kind of fear that plagued me in other places. I imagine it was in part because everyone I met was unfailingly polite. Perhaps, after growing up in Arizona, I felt more at home in the West than I had in other places. But I suspect that much of it had to do with being in Montana—Big Sky Country, they call it, and aptly so. Every evening I'd sit and watch the stars come out, bright as miniature headlights, tens of thousands of them. Every day I spent my time outside in rolling grasslands with horses, dogs, and sheep and the people who cared for them. It was one of the happiest times of my life.

In the end, my hard work and adventures paid off. I was awarded the prestigious Allee Award in 1988 for best graduate student paper at the Animal Behavior Society annual conference. I confirmed that handlers all over the world used similar sounds to speed up and slow down working animals. I tested the hypothesis that these sounds directly influenced behavior on four litters of puppies I raised on the roof of Birge Hall, finding that, indeed, short repeated notes were more effective at teaching pups to come when called than to sit down when asked. Finally, I did nonintrusive neurological tests that showed that, after training, the pup's brains were focused primarily on the number of notes of the signals rather than any other feature.

I had never won anything of any note in my life, and when

my name was called out at the award ceremony, I could barely walk to the stage. I have never felt so honored. But it wasn't the award that stayed with me—it was the importance of clear communication between us and other animals. Then and there, I resolved to make the "most beautiful noises" that I could to all of the animals around me.

# CHAPTER TWELVE

I had imagined that after I got my degree, I would find a job teaching at a small private college somewhere close by. But after my dissertation research, I became more attracted to a life in which I could interact with my two favorite species, people and dogs. Consulting about animals with serious behavior problems allowed me to be a teacher, a social worker, and a woman who got to work with animals all day long—without having to marry a rancher.

In 1988 a friend/colleague and I started a business specializing in solving serious behavior problems in companion dogs. Nancy Rafetto and I knew a lot about behavior, a little about helping people with their dogs, and nothing about running a business. We began by doing house calls and working from our homes, but the late-night phone calls began to wear on us. They came in at all hours. If the problem wasn't "Barry growled at me again, what should I do?" it was "Martha will NOT come into the house when I call her out of the backyard, and I'm missing an important meeting!"

We opened a one-room office in the small town of Black Earth, Wisconsin, about forty minutes' drive from central

Madison. Most people had no idea what we did. We got a lot of calls asking if we groomed poodles. The majority of our clients were referred by veterinarians, happy to send their clients to professionals trained in behavior modification. We soon learned that being an applied animal behaviorist fluctuates on a daily basis between risky and rote, heartwarming and heartbreaking.

My first client was Petunia, a cocker spaniel mix whose owner had just moved to Madison on a Friday and had left Petunia crated up in the new apartment when she went to work the following Monday. She returned to find Petunia's face covered with blood from the wounds she'd received while trying to chew out of her wire crate, and a furious landlord who said the dog had barked continuously all day long. "You've got two days to get the problem solved, or you're out of here," he said.

Petunia had a classic case of separation anxiety, and because her owner had no friends in the area and couldn't take any time off her new job, I spent the next two weeks teaching Petunia that she'd be fine alone in the new apartment while her owner was at work. After settling in with Petunia, I'd get up from the couch, pick up a set of keys, and toss her some treats. Sit back down. Then I'd repeat the sequence—get up, pick up keys, toss treats, sit back down—twenty times. All to teach Petunia that good things happen when someone picks up the keys. Next I'd pick up the keys and take five steps toward the door. Treats to Petunia. Then pick up the keys, walk all the way to the door, put my hand on the doorknob. Petunia would get chicken. Eventually, I'd leave the apartment for thirty seconds, then one minute, then ten, while Petunia sucked food out of a hollow toy. These steps conditioned Petunia to feel good instead of panicked when her owner left the apartment. They also taught me a lot about the patience and stamina required to turn around separation anxiety.

It took two weeks and about seventy hours of my time, but Petunia learned to be comfortable while her owner was at work. I think I charged the client a total of $150, and I didn't bill for either driving expenses or travel time. But the vet who made the referral was impressed, and that case led to another case, which led to three more. Before long, Nancy and I had a full-time caseload. After a few years, Nancy left to take a position at the university that was more likely to pay for her daughter's love of horses, but I kept with it. I had caught the bug and loved acting as a translator between members of two different species.

· · · · ·

As I worked, I channeled my idol, Jane Goodall, and saw myself as a field ethologist working in living rooms instead of the forests of Africa. I watched dogs as if recording the behavior of a wild species, carefully observing every change in eye expression or twitch of the lips. Once you are an experienced observer, you know that dogs are always trying to talk to you; you just need to pay attention.

I quickly learned what every good trainer and behaviorist knows: Dogs have a silent voice that is easy to hear, but most people don't know how to listen. Dog owners often need a translator, no matter how much they love their dogs. Teaching them how to communicate with their dogs was my primary responsibility. Though understanding what a dog is trying to tell you is not rocket science, it seems not to be intuitive, either. Mostly, you listen with your eyes.

When I taught dog training classes, I'd have an owner practice a difficult recall, perhaps calling the dog away from food held in an assistant's hand. The class would watch the owner praise her dog when it responded correctly, and I'd ask the rest of the class to describe how the dog responded to hearing "Good boy, Bailey!" and getting pats on the head. Consistently, observers would say that the owner's reinforcement had been successful. "She was so cheerful!" they'd say. "Great job." However, when I would ask how the dog had responded, the observers would realize that they hadn't been watching the dog at all; they'd been watching the owner.

We'd repeat the exercise, and this time they'd notice that Bailey would turn away while being petted on the head and try to avoid his owner's hand. Did Bailey like the petting and the praise? "No!" the class would answer, like a surprised Greek chorus. I suggested that the "slap, slap" variety of head pats are disliked by most dogs and made Bailey *less* likely to come when called, not more so. Next we'd watch the dog's response when he got a piece of dried chicken for running to his owner on cue, and this time Bailey would dance a happy dance while looking directly into his owner's eyes: "Yes! I like this game. Can we do it again?"

The same phenomenon—a dog clearly communicating something unnoticed by his owner—happened in my office on a daily basis. Max would creep into my office while the owners said, "Oh, he's fine. Go ahead and pet him!" Meanwhile, Max would stand silent and still, eyes round in fear, begging me to please, please, please, not come over and lay my foreign hands on his body. If he had been a person, he would have been whimpering. Or crying.

I loved playing Dr. Dolittle and acting as a bridge between individuals of two species who might adore each other but often miscommunicate. However, it wasn't always easy.

• • • • •

I hadn't seen many clients when a dog named Tanker came into my office. Tanker was a big, brilliant border collie who bit people. By the time I saw him, he had quite a record under his collar. When he was eight months old, he bit the mailman. He bit the vet with the commitment and consistency of a sports fanatic. And lately, he'd bitten his owner, George, who sat in my office with tears in his eyes, explaining to me how much he loved Tanker and how he hoped I could help him.

George sat with his wife, Cynthia, shuffling his feet as he talked, the scuff of his leather shoes on the carpet repeating like a quiet drum underneath his words. I was listening, but I kept my eyes on Tanker—it seemed wise, under the circumstances. The dog, absolutely huge for a border collie, lay at George's feet, sizing me up with steely eyes. George's eyes were soft as he told me how much he loved his dog, even though Tanker growled when he tried to brush him and had bitten him the night before when George reached out to stroke his head.

Tanker loved to cuddle up in bed beside George and Cynthia. He tended to sleep on George's side—no doubt because there was a lot more room. Cynthia was as large as George was small. She was at least five-eleven and broad of beam. George was rail-thin and couldn't have been more than five-six. Listening to them talk that summer afternoon, I couldn't keep the "Jack Sprat" nursery rhyme out of my head.

Cynthia's laugh was as big as her body, and she used it often when interrupting George to tell her version of the story. "Smartest dog I've ever had," she said. "Tanker's got George wrapped around his little finger. I can't convince George that he has to take charge, you know, be the alpha. That's why we came to you. I thought he'd listen to you better than to me. We both love Tanker, but I know this is getting serious, and I can't stand to see him push George around." She turned her head from me to her husband and said, "George? Show her what he does when you reach to brush him."

George dug the dog brush out of the voluminous bag Cynthia had carted in, eased off his chair, and sat down next to Tanker. He reached toward Tanker with the brush.

There was no mistaking the low growl that emanated from the dog's throat. Tanker's body stiffened and his mouth closed. He turned his head to stare at George's hand. The white patch of fur around Tanker's muzzle accentuated the tiny crinkles in his lips as he started to snarl.

"Show her, George. Show her how he'll snap at you."

George paused and examined the hairbrush. It had a worn backing and plastic bristles. The office was silent again for a moment. All I could hear was the wall clock ticking down the seconds, and the sound of Tanker's quiet breathing. I quietly suggested that perhaps I could be the one doing the reaching, but George responded by reaching forward and touching the brush to Tanker's back. Tanker's head swung around so fast it barely seemed to move. First it was facing left and then, seemingly instantaneously, it was facing right. His teeth clamped on the brush with a clacking sound as George pulled back and yelled, "NO!"

"See what I mean?" Cynthia said. "He's getting really dangerous."

"Getting dangerous" was a pallid description of a dog who had bitten multiple times. I played with my pen.

"Tanker is such a good dog in so many ways," George said. "He's so smart, he even makes up his own games! He's started running up the stairs and dropping a ball so he can chase it and catch it when it gets to the bottom. Then he picks it up and runs back up to the top and starts again. Can you imagine?"

When people tell me their dog is smart, I usually say, "I'm so sorry." I'd learned early on that smart dogs turn into problem dogs as often as not. It doesn't work out so well when the dog is a better trainer than the owner, and in spite of our species' ability to invent chocolate and duct tape, that's not uncommon. Put a dog and a human in a room for two hours, and I'll guarantee you the dog will have done most of the training.

"Most of the time, Tanker is so loving. We'd hoped for him to be a therapy dog—you know, the kind you take to nursing homes to cheer up the patients. He's such a wonderful dog, at least most of the time, and he just loves people. We thought he'd be comforting to so many people if only he didn't bite. Do you think you can help him?" George asked.

Help *him*? At that point I was thinking more about helping myself. It was time for me do a hands-on evaluation. Working directly with a dog is the behavioral equivalent of a physician doing an exam in a medical clinic. You just don't know what's going on until you can interact with the dog yourself. But Tanker was not a dog I wanted to deal with that afternoon. It was early in my career, and I hadn't been working with aggressive dogs for very long. In addition, I was exhausted. I'd already seen three clients before Tanker came in, and recurring nightmares had kept me up much of the night. I had begun to dream repeatedly about being mauled by a pack of dogs after an eighty-pound mixed-breed dog had wrapped his teeth around my hand (my fault). I'd wake up screaming, images of huge, jagged teeth ripping into me as I lay helpless on my back.

After a few months of this, I decided my brain and body were trying to reconcile the reality of working with aggressive dogs. I began to make friends with teeth: "Oh, Charlie," I'd say, "what big teeth you have! They are SO shiny and white!" The dreams went away, and after a while I became comfortable working with animals who had carpet knives in their mouths and were willing to use them. It didn't occur to me at the time how important it was to find a way to face fear in an environment where I had knowledge and control on my side.

Tanker was giving me an opportunity to test that out. He was lying at Cynthia's feet, staring straight into my eyes with the kind of look Dirty Harry threw the bad guys before the fight started. I knew I couldn't skip working directly with him. It's one thing to talk to clients about how their dogs behave, but it's another thing to see it for yourself. "Well," I said as I got up from my chair, "I can't give you any guarantees about what we can accomplish, but I can say that most dogs can be helped. It's just impossible to know how much better they can get until you start them on a treatment plan." I looked at Cynthia and said, "Before I can answer George's question, I need to work with Tanker a bit. Is that all right?"

"He's all yours, hon," said Cynthia. "Do be careful, though— he's awfully fast."

I looked at Tanker, who continued to look straight into my eyes. I took a breath.

Grabbing a handful of treats, I stood up and went halfway across the room. "Hey, Tanker," I crooned, cocking my head sideways and waving a treat in my hand. Tanker cocked his head and bumped the end of his tail twice on the ground. Thump, thump.

I smooched and patted my leg. Tanker got to his feet and walked toward me, wagging his tail slowly. There was nothing friendly about this wag. Tail wags are like smiles—usually, they indicate friendliness, but not always. You know those movies in which the hit man smiles right before he pulls the trigger? Or the glassy smile of someone who disses you in front of your date at a cocktail party? Tanker's tail wag was somewhere in between the look of a cold-blooded killer and a rude sneer from a rival.

"Tanker, sit," I said, sweeping my right hand up as a visual signal. Tanker plopped his butt down on the carpet enthusiastically. Apparently, that was a game he was happy to play. Cynthia and George laughed. "Isn't he cute?" she said.

"Good boy, cutie," I said, and tossed him a treat. He snatched it out of the air like a sea lion in a circus and wheeled back toward me. He'd gotten up to grab the treat, so I asked for a sit again. Wham, he slammed his hindquarters down, raised a right paw up like a salute, and cocked his head. I got the distinct impression he was enjoying himself. Cynthia and George practically liquefied with love.

"Good boy, Tanker." I moved forward one step. "Lie down," I told him quietly, pointing toward the ground.

Tanker's mouth closed and, ever so slightly, his body stiffened. Damn. I moved to his side, showed him the treat in my right hand, and eased it down toward the carpet as I softly said, "Lie down."

Tanker turned his head and glared into my eyes with a look that almost stopped my heart. Until then, I had not felt the meaning of the phrase "my blood ran cold." It's not just that you stop breathing or feel a rush of adrenaline that makes your stomach clench and your heart race. It's all that, yes, but your insides cool off in a way that has nothing to do with the weather. Tanker's eyes went still and steely, as if to remind me that he was armed, cocked, and loaded, with teeth designed to rip open leather. This look needed no analysis—my body knew exactly what it meant and started broadcasting trouble like the "engine overheating" light that blinks on your dashboard.

I took another approach. I cooed. I showed Tanker the treat again, said, "Awww, too bad," and popped it into my mouth. It was dried fish from Alaska. It tasted absolutely horrible.

"Ummm, so good!" I said, smiling smugly as I chewed the hateful stuff. George was watching this performance with rounded eyes. Cynthia guffawed and then slapped George on the thigh.

"That'll fry his eggs!" Cynthia chortled. George smiled but looked confused.

So did Tanker. He continued to stare at me, but his gaze had softened. He was giving me his full attention, waiting for what would come next. That seemed like a good start, so I was encouraged to continue.

I showed him another treat, lured him to the floor with it in one fluid motion, and said, "Lie down." Tanker looked at the treat, about twelve inches below his mouth, his eyes riveted on the food in my hand. My own were glued to his shoulder, watching for signs that he'd lunge to bite my hand. George and Cynthia were silent, and I could feel their focused attention without looking at them. The absence of breathing in the room was broken by the afternoon train whistling through town a few blocks away.

Tanker didn't lie down. "Too bad," I said, and withdrew the treat again. This time I only pretended to eat it; I palmed it and put it in a pocket. Tanker stood up and walked to within a foot of me. He raised his head to make eye contact with me again, and again I heard a growl. He kept his eyes locked directly on mine and walked one stiff step toward me. "Give me the treat, bitch"—dogs can say that, just not out loud—"or I'll bite you."

Great. Now what? Stay loose; I knew how important that was, so I took some deep breaths and softened my posture—not an easy task when my heart was pounding so hard I could feel it on the inside of my rib cage. I was scared, no question. The more important question was whether that was equally obvious to Tanker.

Probably. I hadn't run into a lot of dogs who had bitten twelve times. I'd had enough experience, however, to know that I was in danger at the moment and could get myself bitten with the smallest of mistakes. I was equally sure that I could get out of this fix by giving up and moving back behind my desk. I glanced at it: an old mahogany ocean liner that I'd picked up for a hundred bucks. It looked like a bunker that I could hide behind before the bombs fell.

But there were Cynthia and George, waiting expectantly for me to provide the magical cure to their problems. And there was Tanker, up close and personal, patiently awaiting my next move.

Keeping my head still, my breathing measured, and my eyes averted, I tossed a treat behind Tanker with a flick of my wrist. We all watched it arch through the air, and saw the white tip of Tanker's muzzle follow it up and around behind his body. He looked back at me momentarily, straight into my eyes, before he turned around and swiped the piece of chicken off the floor with a fat pink tongue.

As he turned away, I let out a breath and stole a glance at Cynthia and George. They had their eyes on Tanker. George's head was cocked, seemingly charmed by Tanker's ability to slurp food off the worn carpet. Cynthia sat and stared, first at him, then at me. I licked my lips and took another breath.

Next round. What I wanted to try next involved getting down

on the ground with my face square in the middle of Tanker's strike zone. I didn't like this plan, but at the time it seemed to be the best option. Soon after working with Tanker, I learned safer and easier ways to handle similar situations, but then it was all I could think of to do. I knew the outcome of this moment was critical. If I could teach Tanker that it was fun to do what I asked, we could begin to turn things around between him, Cynthia, and George.

"Hey, handsome!" I said, determinedly chipper. Tanker turned around to look back at me, and I swear he looked amused. He came closer and watched me take a piece of chicken out of the canvas treat pouch that I wore around my waist. I held the treat in my right hand and showed it to him. As his nose began to twitch in response, I asked him to sit again. After he did, I crouched down on one knee and extended my other leg parallel to the ground, about eighteen inches high.

Then I moved the treat down toward the floor, on the other side of my extended leg. In order to get it, Tanker would have to lie down and crawl partway under my outstretched leg to get the treat. I didn't ask him to do anything; I just concentrated on holding my leg out straight and the treat in place and avoided looking directly into his eyes. He tried standing up as if to lean over my leg and get the treat, but I just withdrew it and asked for a sit again. He sat. Good start. I teased him again with the treat by holding it under my leg. Like a carrot pulling a donkey forward, I lured him so that he had to lie down first in order to get the treat.

You can count on one hand the number of dogs who don't lust after chicken. Tanker, luckily, was not one of them. A thin stream of drool coalesced on the side of his mouth. The food was still two inches away. All eyes were on his head as he finally crouched down on his forelegs to try to get the food.

I cooed, "Good boy!" and released the food into his mouth, rewarding him for going down toward the ground, even if not all the way.

I got him back into a sitting position and lured him downward once again. After a long hesitation, Tanker lay down flat on the ground. "Yes! What a good boy you are!" I crowed, giving him several more pieces of chicken from my pouch.

"See, isn't he clever?" George said.

"A food hound is more like it," Cynthia answered, but she was smiling.

Tanker and I repeated the exercise a few times, until it began to feel like a game—hopefully to him as much as to me. Of course, I hadn't really asked him to do anything; I was merely finding a way to get him to lie down in my presence. On our fourth try, he began lying down without hesitation, and I said, "Lie down," right before he collapsed his forequarters to the ground. On the seventh try, I said, "Lie down," with the food in front of my leg. He didn't have to lie down to get the food, but as I'd hoped, he did anyway. The next time I stopped extending my leg and stayed squatted down beside him. Good thing, too; my thigh muscles had been screaming for the last several minutes.

He lay down. Glory hallelujah, he lay down just because I asked him to. I gave him the rest of my chicken and walked to my desk, trying not to dive behind it. My legs were shaking, no doubt from the effort of squatting on one and extending the other.

Once I was settled, we talked for a long time about how Tanker needed to learn that it was fun to do what they asked; they had to find fun and friendly ways to influence his mind, rather than trying to force him to be obedient. They both burst out laughing when I suggested George start spoiling Cynthia more than the dog. Cynthia liked the idea of using Tanker's brilliance to shape the right behavior, and we worked out a set of exercises for the next few weeks. They agreed to come back in two weeks.

When they left, I wasn't optimistic. One-trial learners like Tanker can be exhausting to train—give the dog a treat just once after he barks and you have a nonstop vocalist. Bring him back inside right after he potties in the backyard, and he learns to delay urinating outside in order to spend more time in the great outdoors. Tanker was smart, no question about it. As it turned out, so were Cynthia and George. They were equally dedicated and became two of my best and most beloved clients. Tanker stopped biting and used his brainpower for good, and their visits became social ones when they traveled to vacation spots in northern Wisconsin.

Cynthia died of cancer a few years later. George told me that he didn't know how he would have made it without Tanker cuddled up beside him through the dark of the night.

· · · · ·

After seeing Tanker, I worked with hundreds of dogs for behavior labeled as aggression. Some dogs were "aggressive dogs" simply because they'd learned that showing their teeth got them what they wanted. They didn't want to hurt anyone; they just wanted what they wanted and had figured out that threats were effective. That was Tanker. But most dogs are "aggressive" because they are fearful. Like Samantha, a spaniel/something-or-other cross who sat in my office like a furry stick of dynamite with a lit fuse. Her owners said, "Oh, she's fine! Go ahead and pet her," while she stood motionless, flicking out her tongue and turning her head away. She was saying in the only language she had,

"Do not reach over and touch me. Not now, just not now." Like unprepared students in a classroom, dogs avoid eye contact when they want to disappear and avoid interactions. Forcing yourself on them rarely leads to something good.

Other dogs barreled into my office frenetically, like job candidates who can't stop talking at an interview. Their owners would laugh while the dogs bounced from wall to wall like hyperactive beach balls. One massive Labrador leaped onto my desk, smashing into my computer, scattering papers like leaves in an autumn storm. "He's so friendly!" the owners chortled. He didn't look friendly to me, he looked frantic. Dogs can express fear in a multitude of ways, from growling in the corner, to standing as motionless as a stuffed dog, to being hysterically active. Dogs are often trying to tell us how frightened they are, but people can be resistant to that. "He's just being dominant," they say about a terrier who is terrified of strangers who loom over her head. "She has a mind of her own!" I'd hear on a weekly basis about a collie who resisted going into a crate during the day because she was frightened to be alone.

But why wouldn't dogs be afraid? They are small compared to us. They have little power. We control their food, their social interactions, and when they are allowed to go to the bathroom. Most important, they have no voice. They can't say, "Please don't grab my head and loom over me while staring straight into my eyes." Or "I'm terrified of that dog walking straight toward me, and the leash and the sidewalk are forcing the two of us into a rude, inappropriate greeting that we would both avoid if you would let us." So they do the only thing they can do: Some dogs cower or try to hide, but others act on their fears by growling or shouting out frightened barks, their ears flattened, the corners of their mouths pulled back in a fear grimace.

I loved them, all of them, especially the fearful, frightened ones who desperately needed someone to hear them, to understand, to have some sense of what they were going through. My empathy for them overrode my own fears of getting bitten, along with my own need to face fear in a context I could control. Dogs can be muzzled. People can't.

# CHAPTER THIRTEEN

As the pale light of a winter sunrise filtered through the window, I heard the first of the black-capped chickadee's spring song: "Woo-HEE, Woo-HEE!" Winter residents like chickadees and cardinals begin to sing when the daylight expands in February, regardless of the temperature. I declare it spring when I first hear those liquid notes, snow and ice be damned.

I padded over to Pippy Tay, sound asleep in the dog bed under the window. "Pippy. Pippy, wake up, hon." Nothing. I said her name again, louder, and gently rubbed her shoulder. She seemed less responsive than ever. Was she breathing?

"PIPPY!" I was yelling now. "Wake up, Pippy!" I shook her shoulder, tears forming in my eyes, the thought that she had died in the night hardening inside of me like the icicles hanging from the gutters. And then she blinked and lifted her head. Her tail began to thump, thump, thump while the tears streamed down my face in relief.

Pip had been the easiest and sweetest of all the dogs I'd ever had. She loved everyone, both two- and four-legged. She may have been a failure as a sheepdog, but she was the ultimate nanny dog, and I didn't want the Peter Pan story to end.

After we got downstairs, I took her outside to potty, being careful to keep her from slipping on the icy driveway. Pippy squatted to pee, and as her body rose back up, she began to shake and twitch. Her back legs collapsed and she sank toward the snow-covered ground, body leaning like a sinking ship, while her head swung around drunkenly. I ran to her and eased her down, checking her eyes for the obvious signs of vestibular disease, a distressing but usually temporary glitch in the inner ear that brings on the symptoms of vertigo. It looks awful and is clearly distressing to the dog, but it tends to disappear within days or weeks. If it were vestibular, Pippy's eyes would be darting back and forth, left-right-left-right. No such luck. I scooped her up, no small task, and carried her into the house. Later that morning, Pippy seemed to have recovered, and veterinarian Dr. John couldn't find anything wrong with her, except that she was well over sixteen, totally deaf, and partially blind.

She had another event a few days later and grew even weaker. Jim and I stopped leaving her alone for fear that she'd get worse and suffer a long, frightening death. We became slaves to the calendar. "Can you take Monday afternoon if I do the morning and our friend Barbara does Tuesday?" By the end of the week, it became clear that it was time. Keeping Pippy alive was just that: Keeping Pippy Alive. I was reminded of my mother in the last year of her life, when she said, "My body is nothing but a burden now. I just want to let it go."

We decided to let Pippy go on a Sunday afternoon. Dr. John agreed to come out and send her off after a celebration of her life. My final arrangements related to the other dogs. Lassie and Tulip could wait quietly in the study while we said good-bye to Pippy in the living room. But Willie? A bundle of adolescent exuberance, he needed exercise and attention, while I wanted a quiet weekend with my dear old friend. A good neighbor with ample room and lots of frisky border collies kindly agreed to take him for the weekend.

Pippy died with her mouth full of chicken and her belly being rubbed. After she was gone, we brought Lassie and Tulip in. We spent slow, bittersweet hours sitting beside Pip's body, trying to bridge the gap between "Pippy here" and "Pippy gone."

We drove her body to the vet clinic the next morning. They had agreed to store her in their freezer until the ground defrosted enough for a burial at the farm. We placed her still-warm, bundled body into the white mist of the freezer and said good-bye again. That was when the full impact of her death hit me hardest. My legs buckled as I turned to leave, and I slumped to the ground, as surprised as everyone else that my body had simply collapsed. My God, it hurts to let a dog go.

· · · · ·

Afterward, Jim and I drove directly from the vet's to pick up Willie, who grinned and leaped and twisted his body in circles of happiness. Except he did it on three legs. He couldn't put any weight on his left foreleg at all, having slipped badly on the ice. Our friend felt sick about it, as if somehow it had been her fault. We reassured her that of course it wasn't, and thank-you-thank-you-thank-you for taking Willie while we said good-bye to Pippy.

I sobbed all the way home, great gulping sobs that took over my body like an alien. I had just gone through two years of extreme medical care for three geriatric dogs, and it wasn't over. Tulip still needed a tremendous amount of care. Lassie's recurrent bladder infections were driving me and her vet crazy. Having just lost a dog whom I had loved and admired for sixteen years, I was wracked with grief. Yet I was also relieved; living for so long with worries about Pippy had been exhausting. Though I desperately needed a respite, Willie's behavioral problems required constant energy and attention.

Every time Willie startled at the slightest noise, bursting upward as if propelled by his panicked barking, I jumped even higher. He'd run wild-eyed to the window while I stood trembling in the living room, attempting to breathe. I'd try to say, "It's okay, Willie; false alarm," in a calm, low voice instead of a fear-filled squeaky one. For years it had been things that came out of the blue—abrupt loud noises or shocking scenes in a movie—that set my heart racing and readied my body to fight for its life. I'd been so much better the last few years; better, that is, until Willie came and made me worse than I'd ever been.

Driving home in the car that morning, I knew instantly that Willie's shoulder injury meant a lot of care for a long time to come, and the stress of keeping an especially active and reactive dog quiet for months on end. And so, while we drove through snowy fields as blue-white as the winter sky, I cried my heart out, grieving for the loss of Pippy and sick at heart from the continual and exhausting drama that was Willie.

# CHAPTER FOURTEEN

Spring was now in full swing on the farm, although it was late in coming. The sunburst honey locust tree unfurled its chartreuse leaves a full month later than usual. The blue-winged warbler should have been singing in the woods across the road. Every spring I heard its unmusical, raspberry-like song, and it always made me smile. I missed it and wondered if it would ever arrive.

As I did now every day on the way home from working with clients, I let my car coast down the hill on the county road that approached the farm, and tried to leave the day's challenges behind me. Some days were easy. I saw a lot of cases that were relatively routine: Young couples needed advice about how to prepare their docile dog for the baby scheduled to arrive in a few months. Other clients had dogs who were afraid of loud noises. After taking a history and getting to know the dog a bit, I explained how to match up something the dog loved with a low-intensity version of what scared it. Once dogs learn that a baby's cries or the sound of thunder leads to eating chicken, their attitude can change quickly. You have to do it right, and in the right order, but the basics of what is called "counter-classical conditioning" are the same in all cases.

Other days, I felt as though my clients and their dogs drove home with me. I'd arrive at the farm heartbroken about someone sobbing in my office because he thought he might have to put down his beloved companion. That particular day I'd met a lunky black Labrador named Marvin who had been a policeman's best friend until the guy married a woman with a three-year-old. The dog had never been around children, and his initial discomfort and attempts at avoidance had changed to outright aggression. The week before I met him, Marvin had bitten the child's face, and now he was beginning to growl at the mother. Tears streamed down the man's face as we discussed their best options, including finding Marvin a new home without children.

I'd seen four clients already, a typical daily load. Each session took from one to two hours, plus another half hour to type up my notes.

After meeting with Marvin, I'd seen a springer spaniel who was so compulsive about eating rocks that he'd had three abdominal surgeries. The veterinarian said she simply couldn't do another surgery with any degree of success, because more scar tissue would impede the natural peristalsis of the intestines. I developed a training routine that included teaching the dog to turn and pick up a toy whenever he looked at a rock, managing him to prevent relapses, and suggesting that they talk to both an Eastern and Western veterinarian about medical treatment for obsessive behavior.

In the early afternoon, a client came in with a large mixed-breed galumpus whose slaphappy attitude around people belied his murderous behavior around other dogs. By the time I saw him, he'd killed the owner's Yorkie and badly injured three other dogs. His owner was older and relatively frail and did not have much money to spend to try to change his behavior, much less contribute to healing the pets her dog had injured. The dog was no spring chicken himself, and the chance of successfully placing him was small. She wept at the realization that I had no magic cure for her and her dog.

After that, a couple entered the office with a small butterscotch-colored dog named Trinket. The man never looked at the woman. The woman never looked at the man. The dog followed suit and lay down under a chair as if exhausted. I asked why they were here and how I could help, although they had indicated when making the appointment that the dog was constantly messing in the house. Silence.

I left my desk to greet Trinket, who wagged weakly at my approach. I got out some treats and began to play games with her. A rescued bichon-poodle mix, Trinket had spent her life pumping out puppies in a puppy mill. She perked up as we went through the basics of sit, lie down, and stay, all rewarded with tiny food treats. She folded her ears and licked my hand when I handled her, quick to learn and caramel-colored cute. I sat back, looked directly at the wife, Diane, and said, "Well, you're not here because she's dumb. She's as smart as she is adorable! But I understand you're having some problems with house-training?"

Diane burst into tears. Harold, her husband, explained that Trinket urinated and defecated all over the house. Whenever she was left in her crate, she pooped in it and got covered in filth. Every time they returned to the house, they had to pull her out and bathe her. Every morning they awoke to find waste in the crate, on the carpet, or in their bed. They told me that they had tried "everything," and now Harold was done with it, sick of the whole mess. He wanted to return her to the rescue group that had pulled her from the puppy mill or to euthanize her. But Diane loved Trinket and couldn't bear the idea of giving her up. They'd been fighting about the dog ever since they got her, and they were both angry and tired. Harold was considering a divorce.

At that, Diane and Harold began arguing in my office, no doubt replaying the same argument they'd been having for months. I interrupted gently and asked if it would be helpful for me to explain what might be causing the problem in the first place. Then we could talk about treatment and the probability of success. They nodded.

Trinket had lived in a small wire crate for years and was never let out except to be bred so that she could produce puppies. She had learned to potty where she slept and to ignore the most basic of canine instincts—to keep her own nest clean. It also appeared that she was suffering from separation anxiety, having lived in a room with other dogs all her life. She may not have had a chance to interact with them, but she had never been truly alone, as she was when Diane and Harold left for work.

The good news was that they hadn't really done everything; there was a lot they could still do to turn things around. Trinket would need to be taught to potty as if she were a puppy—going outside every few minutes and getting a special treat for eliminating outside. Diane and Harold needed to use commercial products that eliminated the scent of urine on the carpet, so that Trinket no longer categorized the house as a bathroom. Her separation anxiety could be treated with the step-by-step plan I had used with Petunia. The bad news was that dogs from puppy mills, especially small ones like Trinket, can't always be fully house-trained. We could make it much, much better. I couldn't guarantee that she would ever be perfectly behaved, but I'd do everything I could in my power to help all three of them.

That was great news for Diane. Not so for Harold, who clearly loved Diane and wanted to love Trinket but was emotionally exhausted by the dog's behavior problems. This is a common scenario for behaviorists and trainers: People often don't come to see us until they are so depleted by the problem that they have little or no energy left for a treatment plan. I learned early on that my job wasn't just to tell owners how they could solve or manage the problem; it was also to help them think through how much energy they had to do so.

Diane began to cry again. Harold tried to hold it together, rubbing his hands as if to wash himself of worries. Trinket sat between them, her eyes questioning.

We talked for a while about how to treat both issues, house soiling and separation anxiety. I gave them my home phone number and told them to call any time. I picked up Trinket and sat her in my lap, stroked the fur between her eyes, and tried to communicate to her that she was loved and possibly would be better understood. They left, Trinket in Diane's arms, Harold shaking my hand and thanking me for my advice.

I was deeply tired as my car turned into the driveway to the farm. When I became a canine applied behaviorist, I had been warned that I would spend most of my time on aggression issues. I'd expected some danger and that I might get bitten a time or two, but I could also minimize the chances of being injured through knowledge and careful planning. But I was not prepared for the emotional toll of "Do I have to kill or rehome my dog?" cases day after day, week after week. After the day I'd just had, I wanted only to take a long, leisurely walk in the woods with my dogs and not to worry about behavioral problems of any kind.

When I got home, I did the chores and then put Willie through his third daily set of exercises designed to heal the torn tendon in his shoulder. Then I gathered up his favorite treats and toys and drove to a local park where dogs were allowed on-leash. While Willie's injury was healing, we were to begin short on-leash walks to start him moving again. The park's leash restrictions also meant that we could safely work on conditioning Willie to be more comfortable around other dogs, because they wouldn't be able to run up into his face. As we began walking across the grass, Willie turned to his left and burst out barking, his voice high-pitched with panic. I jumped, heart racing. Knowing full well that my reaction would only worsen Willie's—and sick at heart that perhaps my own problems had created some of Willie's—I took two long breaths to calm myself down.

When I turned to assess the "threat," I expected to see an approaching dog, but it was only a tall man ambling along behind us, clearly out for a relaxing walk. No dog; just a guy. He wore a hat that made him look even taller. Willie kept up his barking as the man got closer. I tried to ignore Willie's noisy agitation, which was like trying to ignore a machine gun going off in my ear. I asked Willie to sit while I gathered myself. "Oh boy!" I managed to say, trying for a happy voice as we played the game we usually did when he saw unfamiliar dogs. I gave Willie a treat when he looked back at me to condition an association between approaching men and things he loved.

I felt hollow. Now Willie had another problem—the fear of unfamiliar men. Willie had always loved people, but as I calmed us both, I realized that he had backed away from the deliveryman the week before. He had also barked atypically at a male friend who came to visit the day after. I gathered what little stamina I had left and moved on, trying to focus on why we'd come to the park—to work on his fear of unfamiliar dogs.

"Watch!" I said to Willie as his head turned toward a West Highland terrier we encountered after the man passed us by. Willie turned his head toward me instead of growling at the other dog, and got a treat. Again I said, "Watch," treated him for his appropriate response, and then let him turn his head back toward the Westie. This time I waited in the hope that he'd turn his head to me on his own, the "auto watch" we'd worked on before that taught Willie to associate seeing other dogs with feeling good, instead of responding to them as if they were serial killers bent on slaughtering us both.

Willie began to turn his head to me as the Westie moved away, but before I could pop the treat in his mouth, three off-leash hounds ran boisterously toward us. Willie exploded—and I couldn't blame him. Asking him to stay calm when he was surrounded by three large barking dogs was like asking an eight-year-old to do calculus at a water park. I put Willie in the car, drove to a quieter spot, and tried again. I got in a few good sessions when the other dogs were far enough away and no tall men frightened him, so Willie was able to focus on the treat or the toy. Finally, as darkness fell, I drove home, exhausted.

I gave Willie a chance to potty before entering the house, but he didn't take it. I went into the kitchen and cobbled together an easy dinner for one, since Jim was out. As I sat down to eat, I smelled the acrid and oh-so-familiar smell of doggy diarrhea. The stress at the park had been too much for Willie, and he had anointed the living room carpet with liquid brown puddles.

"Damn it, Willie!" I said. I'd like to say that I spoke quietly, but I didn't. There were multiple reasons not to correct him at all—he couldn't help it, it was too late, he was already stressed—

but my words were not helpful in any way. They were simply an expression of my own exhaustion and frustration. I thought of Harold, how much he loved Diane and wanted to love Trinket, and yet how deeply tired he was by the constant conflict. He wanted a respite when he came home, not another difficult challenge. So did I, and I knew that losing my temper and yelling at Willie was the worst thing I could do. But I did it because my exhaustion overwhelmed my reason and knowledge.

Willie's problems seemed never-ending. His shoulder was healing, but he needed physical therapy and careful monitoring of his activity levels: not so easy to do with a dog who could twirl in a full circle before you could even get a word out. If I let my guard down for a fraction of a second, Willie could destroy all the healing that had occurred in the weeks before. It was like watching a single popcorn seed in a hot, oily pan and trying to pull it out just before it popped. All day, every day.

Willie's fear of other dogs also required energy and attention in order to counteract it. We weren't close to "done" yet, as the off-leash dogs at the park had proved. Left free in the house, he barked desperately at the window—eyes hard, saliva flying—when someone walked a dog down the road. He panicked if an unfamiliar dog got closer than twenty feet. These events rarely happened because I managed him so carefully. Now I needed to add the same kind of conditioning program to teach Willie to associate unfamiliar men with something wonderful. I knew exactly what to do, but I also knew it would take time and energy to pull it off.

· · · · ·

Energy was in short supply that night. After yelling at Willie for doing something he couldn't help, I added shame and regret to anger and exhaustion. I cleaned up the mess, threw my dinner down the garbage disposal, and went to bed. Jim came out to the farm later that night and cuddled next to me. I listened to him breathing beside me all night, until the sky began to lighten and the wrens welcomed the day with their rock sonata of song.

# CHAPTER FIFTEEN

Willie's shoulder improved, and then it didn't. Every time it seemed that he had fully recovered, a setback would occur. It didn't help that he had matured into an exceptionally long and tall border collie, looking like a marathoner who gave up his running shorts to play professional soccer. Sheepdogs have to run great distances, but much of their work is like that of a quarter horse and involves slamming their legs into the ground to turn right or left at high speed to work the stock. As much as he loved it, Willie wasn't built for it.

But it wasn't working sheep that caused Willie his most serious injury. A visiting dog slammed into him during play and left him whimpering on three legs. The orthopedic specialist at the University of Wisconsin Veterinary Medical Teaching Hospital said he'd badly torn his bicep tendon in the same shoulder he'd injured earlier. Damage to other connective tissue was also possible. We could try more rest and rehabilitation or do surgery right away. Rest included months of crate rest and leash restrictions; surgery would require even more. It seemed wise to get it dealt with once and for all.

Willie walked into the clinic on the day of his surgery wagging from the shoulders back. He happily limped alongside the technician into the back rooms with just a brief glance at me. The surgeon called me while Willie was opened up on the table to tell me that not only was the bicep tendon torn, but another tendon and two ligaments were also badly damaged. They could not be surgically repaired. There was no way to know if the operation would result in a dog who could ever work sheep again. He might always be permanently disabled. Did I want to go ahead with the surgery anyway? "Yes," I said, sick at heart after hearing the news.

The day after the operation, they brought Willie out to the consulting room, floppy-boned and blank-eyed, a quarter of his body shaved. The surgeon had severed his badly torn bicep tendon, pulled it through a hole that she'd bored into the humerus bone, and screwed it into place. When I saw the radiographs of the screw, I was appalled at its size. It looked big enough to hold up a house.

I sat stroking him, stunned into silence by his frailty, as the surgeon explained the importance of keeping him immobile for weeks in order for the screw to set into the bone. Without the blanket of white fur on his chest and black fur on his shoulder, Willie's skin was soft, velveteen, but mottled like that of a pinto horse. The incision was huge. He seemed so helpless and vulnerable.

I carried him into the car and drove as slowly as traffic would allow. When we arrived home, Jim took over and gently lifted Willie out of the car and placed him in front of his crate. He went into it and slept quietly that night, but the next morning he woke at dawn. When I walked into the room, he greeted me with a grin, a swoosh of the tail, and a 360-degree spin inside the crate. "I'm good! Let's go play!"

Of course, he wasn't. Even the slightest abrupt movement

could destroy the healing process. Willie needed to stay almost immobile for several weeks for his bone to heal. "Immobile" should be listed in the dictionary as the antonym of "young border collies." He was wonderful about his crate—he entered it happily and rarely whined or barked there, but he could still perform an entire gymnastics routine when inside, no matter how small it was. A young border collie won't stay in a crate for long without starting to spin in circles, so I couldn't let down my guard even when he was confined. When he began to move too much, I'd sit beside the crate and use my voice to calm him down. Aware that the words "crate" and "rest" were not compatible, I kept him attached to me on a leash whenever I could. I cooked and ate dinner with him at my side. We watched TV together in the evenings, attached like convicts in a chain gang, serving out our time.

After the first month, Willie's inactivity reduced him to an unnatural calmness. Just as lying around all day makes people tired, Willie became a kind of rug potato, sleeping and walking on-leash with a resigned sluggishness, no doubt in part because I relentlessly reinforced him for moving slowly. But he was still Willie and still alerted to sounds too quiet for anyone else to hear, if they even existed at all. Every time Willie looked ready to leap up, a wave of fear coursed through me. Would he jump at the wrong moment and cause his shoulder to fall apart?

The primitive part of my brain, which turns on the fight-or-flight system, began working overtime. There was never a time at home when I could relax. I was always ready to react at the speed of light in case Willie moved too fast. I began to have trouble sleeping again and became more nervous at night. I stopped walking in the woods at night and took a flashlight to the barn so that I didn't have to walk into the darkness before finding the light switch. Every night when I closed the drapes in the upstairs bedroom, I was afraid there would be a strange man standing under the yard light, staring back at me.

After eight weeks, Willie's bone healed enough that he could begin physical therapy for his muscles, tendons, and ligaments. Jim bought a ramp that allowed me to walk Willie into the car on the way to meet with UW's veterinary rehabilitation specialist, Courtney Arnoldy, twice a week. Between therapy sessions, Willie and I did his exercises religiously, three times a day, a half-hour each, for eight long months. He became a circus dog—balancing on teeter boards, perching on large air-filled balls, striding on the underwater treadmill at the rehabilitation clinic as I lured him forward with treats.

Spring became summer, and summer turned into fall. The sumacs turned the color of blood oranges, the crickets buzzed like baby chain saws, and the starlings chattered as they clustered on the telephone wires. Willie's restrictions and exercise routine continued until, finally, he was allowed to trot. Still on-leash, still highly modulated. At first our homework was: "Walk for ten minutes on-leash, then trot for ten seconds, then walk for two more minutes. See how he does, and increase the trotting up to thirty seconds. We'll evaluate his progress at our next session."

The first time Willie was allowed to trot outside, his head rose up and he looked at me like a little boy who had just discovered ice cream. The second time, he got so excited that he flipped around in a full circle before I could stop him. I called him "Rip Van Willie," after the character who had slept for twenty years and finally woken up.

After I pulled him back from spinning in circles, he turned to face me and looked straight into my eyes. He gave a long, breathy sigh and turned his head away as we walked back and forth down the driveway. He refused to look at me again.

Instead of being encouraged by these short moments of release, he became depressed. Evenings were punctuated by his drawn-out sighs. It was as though each newfound moment of freedom reminded him of what he was missing and made things worse instead of better.

Willie wasn't the only one who was depressed. Keeping him at a slow trot was like trying to convince a sparkler to shine on one side and not the other. I was still on alert 24/7 to avoid Willie tearing his shoulder tissues before they had fully healed. In addition, much of what I loved most in life had been taken away. No working sheep together. No long off-leash walks in the woods. No joyful dog, running free, turning back to look at me: "Are you coming? Hurry up!" I hadn't realized how much of my happiness revolved around our mutual freedom. The recovery process had already stretched over a year. It seemed endless. I counted up the months that Willie had been restricted to his crate or a leash because of his bad shoulder, and realized he'd spent over a third of his life restrained because of injury. During all that time, I couldn't let down my guard for even a moment, lest he set himself back.

I began to see Willie as not so much my therapy dog but the reason I needed therapy myself.

· · · · ·

On the darkest night of that dark time, I lay on the rug, stroking Willie's belly and wishing I hadn't kept him. I hadn't signed up for a dog like Willie. His happy face could open my heart, but his look of cold rage could chill my blood. His cuddly nature bathed me in sweet peace, but he could destroy it all in a second by scrambling up in a panic, sending me to the ceiling and keeping me on edge for the rest of the night.

It was time to face the facts: Willie was not just exhausting me; he was bringing up issues that I thought I'd buried and forgotten years ago.

# Chapter Sixteen

It was late summer 1966. My best friend in high school, Clarisse, and I had enrolled in modeling school. She had gorgeous long legs and a mane of strikingly red hair. I had short, stumpy legs and a thicket of bleached-blond hair, but I got offered a few jobs through the school, including one for an upcoming convention.

A dozen of us teenage-model wannabes had been hired to introduce an auto company's newest cars by prancing like fillies as they rolled onto center stage. I was fifteen and dolled up like a cheerleader in a butt-high red skirt and tight blouse. We were all carrying pom-poms and rehearsing in a coliseum-like building, clustered in a small circle in the middle of an oval arena, miniaturized by the thousands of empty seats rising around us to the top of the building. I worried that my hair would frizz and that the pimple on my chin was not adequately covered with pancake makeup. The girl next to me had perfect skin and lush black hair that she would shake out of her face every few seconds. I narrowed my eyes as she repeated for the fourth time, "What did he say?"

The stage manager had been giving us instructions, looking at his clipboard more often than at us. "Run over here," he said.

"Walk over there. Shake your pom-poms. Can you toss your hair a little bit?" The girl with creamy skin flicked her head, tossing her hair. "Yeah, like that," he said.

He kept talking while we circled around him, trying to catch what he was saying before his words drifted away into the vast open space around us. The only other sounds came from the technicians, who were setting up lights on the catwalk five stories above, occasionally calling to each other.

The two girls across the circle from me had begun giggling at a private joke when someone yelled, "Watch out!" The stage manager grabbed the girl in front of me and pulled her backward. Simultaneously, a life-size dummy fell through the air right above where she had been standing. I clearly remember thinking, *That's not funny.* It had to be a practical joke. My mind was unable to identify the lumpy thing falling through the air as a person. It took a second or two, after he landed just a few feet in front of me, to understand that it wasn't a dummy—it was a living human being.

He hit parallel to the ground, flat on his belly, legs and arms extended. His clothes and his body split upon impact like a watermelon dropped on the pavement. My eyes went first to the split at the back of his jeans, exposing his bright white underwear. My first reaction was embarrassment. I thought, the sentence clear as a scalpel's edge years later, *It's okay, mister, don't be embarrassed; we won't look at your underwear.* It did not occur to me that split pants were not the primary problem. Then I saw that his arms were bare, and they were split open, too. As my brain began to comprehend what was happening, he raised his head and made a gurgling sound. And then he put his head down and died.

Red. Fresh-flowing blood is shockingly red. An expanding fan of it grew from underneath his hips and thighs. The blood spread out in perfect symmetry, flowing fast, a brilliant red triangle between his legs. One of the girls ran over and held his hand, cradled his forehead. Most of us stood transfixed and mute. Helpless.

Within minutes we were herded away, toward the outskirts of the arena. I found a pay phone by a shuttered hot dog stand and groped through my purse for a dime. As it dropped into the coin slot, I heard the wail of an approaching siren.

"Mom? Mom, can you come get me now?"

"What's wrong?" she asked. I wasn't expected to call for a ride home for hours.

"A man fell. I think he's dead. There's blood everywhere. Please can you come and get me now?" I went outside and sat on a cement step to wait for her, sweating in the sun, staring at the empty parking lot.

The next day, my parents and I read an article about it in the newspaper over the bacon and eggs my mother made every morning. A thirty-seven-year-old electrician, married with two children, had fallen fifty-eight feet to his death. We spoke his name and thought with sympathy of his wife and two children. We never talked about it after that; it never occurred to us to do so. I willed myself to forget about it, so that it wouldn't ever bother me again.

• • • • •

But of course it did. Willie's hyperactive startle response made me recognize my own response to things happening "out of the blue." His behavior made me worse, but it also forced me to admit that seeing a man fall out of the sky and die at my feet had created a continuous warning light in my brain. And that signal couldn't be turned off with willpower alone.

# CHAPTER SEVENTEEN

Once a man has fallen out of the sky and died at your feet, your brain stays ready for it to happen again. Willie's reactivity, and my need to react instantly to keep him still and allow him to recover, made me more anxious and fearful than I'd ever been. Many of the fears from which I thought I'd recovered had come back. My startle response had been reset to PANIC. I was having a recurring nightmare that I was standing powerless on a cliff as Willie's uncle Luke fell to his death into a roaring river. Every day as I drove home from the office, I would imagine that the house and the dogs inside had burned to ashes. I would blink and shake my head to try to dispel the image, but it would not leave me until I arrived home at night, gulping air in relief to find the house still standing.

I froze if someone directed a snarky comment at me. I snapped at Jim or the staff in my office when I got frustrated or frazzled. My "best self" became harder to find—it seemed I was either going mute and freezing in the face of disagreements, or I was say-ing something I later regretted. I willed myself to be the person I wanted to be, the person everyone else expected me to be. Much of the time I succeeded, and I adapted to being jumpy, sleep-deprived, and exhausted. But not always. Not often enough.

I was spent. My emotional pockets empty, I had nothing in reserve. Willie had done remarkably well with his restrictions, but a young, exercise-impoverished border collie is like a car with its engine gunning and the brake on. If you don't engage the tires at some point, smoke starts coming out of the pipes. Yet the vets continually reminded me that just one quick movement could destroy all the effort we'd put in so far. "One quick movement" was Willie's middle name.

I startled every time he began to move too fast; I felt as if disaster could strike any moment. I had become so tightly wired that I was the one who jumped first at the slightest noise.

I was tired of teaching him tricks, of trying to keep his mind engaged, of always being ready to anticipate the next leap. Even after all our training, Willie's fear of unfamiliar dogs was extreme. Sometimes it escalated to a chilling level of out-of-control rage. We were making good progress—he was now comfortable seeing other dogs unless they surprised him and came too close too fast—but each step forward took time, patience, and energy. He still overreacted to even the smallest stimulus and was fearful of loud noises or strange shapes.

His challenges to my other dogs over resources had decreased but required constant vigilance. Though he responded well when male visitors threw him treats, I managed his interactions with them obsessively, lest something go wrong and Willie's fear should increase instead of decrease. His digestive system had improved with age, but I had to feed him with obsessive care. He needed Chinese medicine, probiotics, certain kinds of protein, like beef or pork, but not others (heaven forbid I fed him chicken), chiropractic care, three Western-medicine veterinarians, and constant training and conditioning.

. . . . .

Now it was my turn to seek help. As Willie lay at my feet, I called my staff into my office and explained that life with him had become so difficult that I needed advice about what to do next. Spending my days helping clients with dogs who generated lawsuits or cats who put grandmothers in the hospital is not an easy job. Seeking advice about behavior problems in pets is often couched as the trivial pursuit of neurotics done only by the overly entitled. But canine behavior problems can be serious. Life-and-death serious. Wondering if your dog, the one who was your best friend before you got married, is going to bite your three-year-old son is not a trivial question. Living in fear of a hundred-pound dog who has begun stalking you is not something you can ignore. I hadn't known how much my clients' emotional pain and suffering would come home with me every night, like cigarette smoke on my clothing. And when I arrived, there would be my Willie, whose behavioral problems needed a week's worth of physical and emotional energy every evening.

My colleagues listened intently, and one of them said: "Trisha, I know you love Willie, but he has been a nightmare ever since you got him. You work hard every day solving serious behavioral problems; you don't need to go home and begin all over again. Look at you! You're exhausted. That's not fair to you, to him, or to your other dogs."

As a result of our discussion, I made the following plan: I would keep him until his shoulder was fully healed, doing all I could to treat his behavioral problems in the meantime. At that point, I'd reassess how it was going and either keep him or find him a better home. Of course, the question arose: What home would that be? Who would want a dog like Willie? I'd deal with that later if I had to.

The discussion was thoughtful, objective, and familiar, like the talks I had with clients every week. Sometimes owners had to face the fact that a dog was so dangerous it was a public health menace. Other owners had to acknowledge that, as much as they loved their dog, she could never be happy living in fear of a toddler pulling her tail, or in terror of another dog who stalked her through the house like an armed serial killer.

It helped to hear my staff's professional objectivity. But this time it was me and my dog we were talking about. I felt sick to my stomach. How could I even think about not keeping Willie? The dog who moaned when he pressed his head against my neck; whose happy face could only be described as radiant. When Willie was good, he was very, very good, and by now I loved him as much as I'd ever loved any dog. But at his worst, he seemed miserable, living his life on the edge of terror, quick to fall into a rage so extreme he seemed crazy.

I didn't have any of the barriers to effective treatments that my clients had. I knew how to condition dogs to assuage their fear of loud noises; I taught people to do it on a regular basis. Willie's health-related problems were exhausting and expensive but not insurmountable. I had access to the best veterinary care in the country. I'd literally written the book on how to handle a dog who was aggressive to other dogs. I had a raft of dog-loving friends who were happy to introduce their dogs to Willie, or to teach him that unfamiliar men were harbingers of toys and treats instead of fear and danger. I'd seen hundreds of dogs who had caused serious injuries to people or other animals. One client had stitched up a long gash in her own forearm herself, afraid that if she got medical care, her dog would be taken away from her. Willie had never hurt anyone.

But there was something else—something that I hadn't allowed myself to talk about. I was just as jumpy as Willie. While his reactivity set me off, I knew that my own startle response did the same to him. We were living in a vicious circle, each making the other worse. In my heart, I knew that in spite of my professional expertise, my own problems meant I wasn't the ideal owner for Willie.

Heartsick, I leashed Willie, and we went out the door to the car. I put him in a sit/stay behind the car while I hauled the heavy ramp from the backseat and placed it so that he could climb in without jumping and reinjuring his shoulder. It was hard for Willie to sit and stay while I lugged the ramp around. When I turned to Willie to release him, he sat big-eyed and trembling, almost overwhelmed by the energy it took to make himself obey and control his almost-out-of-control impulses. His face was desperate with the need to leap forward—to move move move, oh-please-I-have-to-move—countered by his desire to be a very good dog, the very best dog anyone could ever have.

That was when it hit me: I knew Willie like I knew myself. I knew what it was like to fight the demons inside and still want so badly to be good. To be so fearful that the slightest noise blows you off the ground as if a bomb has gone off under your feet. I knew what it was like to be happy and friendly on the outside and yet spend much of your life in fear.

I looked at his imploring face, and my heart opened up so wide and fast that my knees went weak. As I released Willie from his stay and he climbed into the car, I knew that I could never send him away. I sat beside him while he licked the tears off my cheeks, and I whispered, "I will, I will, I will, Willie, I will move heaven and earth to try to help us both."

# CHAPTER EIGHTEEN

After making my pledge to Willie, I recognized that I was no longer capable of dealing with my problems by myself; I had to get help. I made an appointment with a therapist, Mare Chapman, recommended by friends. Years earlier, before I got Willie, I had benefited immensely from working with Anne Simon Wolf, a brilliant therapist who had helped me relieve much of the guilt and shame I'd felt over the incident with my sister's boyfriend, lodged for decades in my chest like a jagged black dagger. How could I have been so weak when Bruce came into my bedroom? Was it my fault that he did? Had I been flirting with him, and betraying my own sister, without even knowing it?

I had attended the Hoffman Process, a weeklong personal growth retreat that combined journaling, group discussions, and guided meditations to help people get rid of the baggage from their past. It also involved a lot of physical activity, including beating up a pillow, as a symbol of one of your inner demons, for forty-five minutes of nonstop fury. I'd picked up the plastic bat the teacher handed to me and whaled away at the pillow, the physical representation of my shame. I began with gusto, but after ten minutes it seemed that I couldn't possibly continue for a moment longer. Somehow I did, for ten more minutes, then twenty. Eventually I went into a kind of a trance state that connected my mind and body in ways they had never been before. When I was done, I felt lighter, less dense, as if I'd lost weight by adding air between the molecules of my body.

I also examined myself and my own behavior, looking honestly at my negative traits, considering which I had adopted from my parents and which I had developed to rebel against them. My list of negative traits began with "too busy." Busy, busy, busy, that was me. I was running a business that provided fifteen to twenty dog training classes a week, along with numerous consultations for serious behavioral problems of dogs and cats. I had a staff and a set of volunteers to manage. I taught a class at the University of Wisconsin–Madison about the biology and philosophy of human-animal relationships. I cohosted a weekly call-in radio show. I wrote books, gave speeches and two-day seminars around the world, and managed a small farm with twenty sheep, three dogs, a cat, and twelve acres of woods and pasture to take care of. The only part I didn't take care of was me.

Before I participated in the Hoffman Process, I bristled when friends said they were concerned about how little time I had to relax. "I'm not too busy!" I snapped at a concerned friend over lunch one day. "I'm sick of people saying I'm too busy. I am NOT too busy!" Later we laughed about it and began calling "busy" the "b-word."

Through the Process, I began to realize that being so busy all the time was both a reflection of my mother's habits, as well as an avoidance of thinking about the events in my past.

The scientist in me loved the fact that solid research had shown the program to have a long-term positive effect on participants' psychological states. The entire week was exhausting, terrifying, and exhilarating, but it provided a safe place to be brutally honest about who I was in relation to who I wanted to be. I began to forgive myself—for being too busy, too weak, too critical of others, and for what happened with my sister's boyfriend. I brought back fifteen-year-old Trisha and showered her with compassion for being a mixed-up young girl who did her best to handle a difficult situation.

But resolving the guilt about what happened in my bedroom was one thing. Recovering from the visceral trauma of having a man fall through the air and die at my feet was another. Years later, Willie's overly reactive startle response showed me that I hadn't yet recovered from it.

One definition of the word "shock" is "something that jars the mind or emotions as if with a violent unexpected blow." No wonder that for decades, I had sensed a man with a baseball bat behind me, always poised to smash me in the head. I had taken a hit to the head, but not in the way I imagined. Shock is different from the experience of other aversive events because it's a reaction to something unexpected. Unpredictable events are harder to deal with than predictable ones; this knowledge is standard fare to any behaviorist. Until Willie's behavior sent me into a second round of therapy, I hadn't known about the power of what some call "fright." Far more than in the usual use of the word—perhaps as a giggled reaction to a scary story told at a slumber party—fright is a kind of a fugue state in which, according to psychiatrist Guillaume Vaiva, one experiences "a complete absence of affect (neither fear nor anxiety), accompanied by a lack of thought, true loss of words and faced with a reality that seems unbelievable."

It is impossible to use words to fully describe an experience in which all thought and language are taken from you, but having felt that, I am compelled to try. Perhaps the best single word that captures the feeling is "stunned"—a condition in which your very existence is momentarily arrested.

Shock, or what some call fright, can be a better predictor of PTSD, or posttraumatic stress disorder, than the experience of trauma itself. One study found that an "immediate fright reaction" in victims of auto accidents (a quarter of whom developed PTSD) was a better predictor of the symptoms of PTSD than experiencing "fear, helplessness or horror."

As I continued in therapy and did my own research on trauma and fright, I learned that severe shocks can have profound effects on brain function. If your life has proved to be a whack-a-mole game, then your brain wires itself to be on alert at all times. We all have certain expectations about daily life that are so deeply ingrained, we never think about them: That we can walk from our house to our car without being swept up into the air by a large flying predator. That someone will not fall from the sky and die at our feet. Once we experience a shock that changes our perception of everyday order, the most primitive part of our brain gets stuck on red alert. It's a desperate and illogical attempt to be prepared for things that happen so fast one can't possibly be ready for them.

It was my nonverbal, subconscious brain that was affected most by seeing a man's violent and shocking death. Despite my previous attempt at therapy, I couldn't talk my way out of a brain that had been rewired in the most primitive of ways. And it *was* rewired: The brain structure of victims of violent trauma changes significantly. The hypothalamus shrinks, and the amygdala becomes hyperactive.

No amount of willpower was going to change that for me. But I began to understand some of my own fears. The man with the baseball bat was my mind's way of keeping me on constant alert, ready for the next disaster. Dark rooms were perfect places for unexpected shocks, given that I couldn't rely on my eyes to see something coming. Willie's over-the-top startle response exacerbated my rewired brain's attempts to continually be ready to fight or flee. It didn't happen only around Willie.

· · · · ·

One day Jim and I were watching the movie *Angel Heart*. It's a brilliant but horrifically violent film that I should have stopped watching long before the camera focused on the corpse of a young woman, spread-eagled on her back with a triangle of dazzlingly red blood pouring from between her legs. A man had shot her with a pistol as he was raping her with it. I froze in the chair, barely breathing, unblinking, unable to get up and leave. When the movie was over, I couldn't move. At all. When Jim spoke, I didn't answer; didn't turn my head. I could hear him, and I wanted to answer, but I couldn't move or speak. I thought, *This must be what catatonia feels like.*

Jim came over, concerned about my silence, and then I yearned to speak, to tell him I was okay. But no matter what words formed in my brain, my mouth wouldn't move. He called my name, repeated it, picked up my hand, touched my face. The need to communicate became overwhelming, but I still couldn't bridge the gap between the words that formed in my head and the effort required to speak them.

I felt crazy then, teetering at the edge of sanity, appalled that I was literally paralyzed by the shock of the image on the screen. After an eternity of a few minutes, I was able to move my right hand. I began to flap it, trying to make it move as if writing. Jim brought me pen and paper, and I wrote, "FLOWERS"—trying to convey that I wanted to see pictures of flowers. He understood and ran to bring me a photo album. He opened the page to an explosion of bright red tulips. Red. Oh God, not red. My head jerked back and my arms flapped like a baby seal's. I wrote, "BLUE," and he turned the page, and there were peaceful blues and muted shadings of lilac.

"I'm sorry. I'm okay. I'm so sorry." Those were my first words to Jim, and he echoed them back: "I'm so sorry, Trisha, I didn't realize that the movie was so violent. We never should have watched it." He held me, comforted me; we touched and kissed and lay together through the night.

A few days later, I saw my therapist Mare, who helped me figure out why I had responded so dramatically to the movie. She asked me to lie down, take some deep breaths, and relax. "Just breathe, and pay attention to whatever comes into your mind." I lay quiet for several minutes while the air conditioner hummed. Nothing came to me, except an itch on my leg and the thought that I should be having better thoughts.

"Just stay with it," said Mare. "Keep breathing, and tell me what your body has to say."

Gradually, from somewhere, the color red appeared in my consciousness until it was all I could think about. "I'm seeing red," I told Mare. "I don't know why. Why red?"

"Just keep breathing and focus on the red. Don't try to force anything, just let whatever comes into your mind enter when it's ready."

Slowly, the red color coalesced into the fan of blood between the woman's legs in the movie, and then I saw the image of the man who fell at the coliseum and the shockingly red blood flowing out of his body, forming a perfect triangle of color between his legs.

"The Man Who Fell," as I began to call him, was a memory I rarely revisited; I had pushed it into the darkest recesses of my mind. But then Willie came along and showed me that willing myself to forget about it wasn't enough to make it go away.

Mare helped me process the event and to begin healing from it by expressing my compassion for the deceased electrician. I settled into the pillows, my head resting against the wall, and talked to him, telling him how sorry I was that he had died. I said a prayer of compassion to his family: "May you be safe. May you be happy. May you be peaceful."

Later, I hired a detective to find his name, needing to give him an identity, for him to be more than a nameless person. His name was Albert S. McCarthy, and every day for several weeks, I began my day by talking to him.

Talking wasn't enough on its own to reboot my brain from "on alert" to a more normal state, so Mare and I discussed what activities made me calm and happy. Just as I had written the word "FLOWERS" to Jim as the only way to break the spell I'd been in after the movie, I instinctively knew that flowers would help me recover. Like my father, I have always loved plants, almost as much as I love animals.

After the session with Mare, I began to spend as much time gardening as I did with the dogs. Jim shakes his head when I return from yet another visit to the garden center with more purple coneflowers and blazing stars and wild bergamots to plant. And there are never enough daylilies.

I dig compost into the red clay of the farm that ridicules the name of my town, Black Earth. I pull and hack and slice away at weeds while Willie lies on the ground and watches. I push heavy wheelbarrows of dandelions and bad soil into a massive pile of plant debris hidden by some cedar trees. I return to the house tired and sweaty and more grounded than I've ever been.

But it took more than gardening to heal me. I wrote extensively in my journal. I learned to meditate. I did yoga. I booked fewer speaking engagements so I could spend more time at home, walk in the woods, and cultivate flowers.

All of these efforts began to work their magic. Though I was still busy, at least I had begun taking care of myself. But sometimes taking care of yourself means digging even deeper, no matter what is buried in the dirt.

# CHAPTER NINETEEN

Neither Willie nor I followed a neat path to recovery; we each made progress in fits and starts. I continued my therapy with Mare, and Willie saw his physical therapist twice a week for his shoulder. He did his exercises, and I did mine. Willie learned to hold up his right paw for ten seconds, then twenty, to strengthen the muscles that supported his shoulder joint. He became even more adept at balancing on a teeterboard, even when I held one paw off the ground. He walked, ever so slowly, over a bar I held parallel to the ground.

Willie's shoulder finally healed enough that he was able to be a happy young dog again, full of energy and joy and a desire to leap into my face while I was carrying grocery bags, purse, and laptop. We took long walks with friends through fields and forests where he could pick up sticks and beg me to throw them so he could retrieve them.

Now that his shoulder was better, we could go back to working harder on his conditioning around other dogs. We took walks in neighborhoods with busy roads where I knew all the dogs would be on-leash. I whipped out his tug toy if he turned his head to me instead of barking or lunging when another dog appeared. We sat inside the car in areas where other dogs were more likely to be off-leash, and Willie got pieces of chicken every time he looked at one and then looked back at me. After the incident in the dog park when Willie panicked at the sight of an unfamiliar man, I began the same work with visitors of my own species. Male friends came to the farm and threw Willie treats, a routine that he decided was the best game ever.

Gradually, Willie's reaction to the sight of another dog changed from tense apprehension to joyful anticipation. If the dog wasn't too close or moving too fast, Willie would lean toward the corgi or cocker spaniel with a grin and a loose, sweeping tail-wag. Soon he was able to play again with his buddy Sydney, the adolescent Australian shepherd. He found a new friend in Mac, a young border collie who played catch-me-if-you-can games with Willie as the birds sang their spring songs in the high pasture. It worked even faster with men, whom he had loved as a puppy, when Willie learned that visiting men always arrived bearing gifts of food or toys. He ran out to greet them with eyes glistening and tail wagging in a happy circle.

Still, I managed him obsessively, especially around other dogs. Good owners of reactive dogs behave like the security guards of celebrities, continually scanning the environment for potential threats. We have Plan B and Plan C well rehearsed in our minds if Plan A begins to fall apart. I always left the farm with a pocket of treats to throw vigorously at the face of any dog who might come running toward us.

Over the months, Willie improved enough that it was time to let him greet dogs outside his small circle of friends. I had continued Willie's herding lessons once he was healed, asking him to fetch me the sheep from farther and farther away, and teaching him to run clockwise or counterclockwise around the flock in response to a quiet word or whistle. He had made a lot of progress, but we both needed a coach to help us move on to the next level. Right around that time, Julie Hill, a well-known sheepdog trainer and trial competitor, was giving a clinic a few hours away from the farm.

A small sheepdog clinic was the perfect place to expose Willie to close contact with unfamiliar dogs. He'd be distracted from the other dogs by his desire to work the sheep. The other participants would be sympathetic to my problems with Willie—working your dog off-leash while he's running free around prey animals is both humbling and exciting. It bonds sheepdog handlers together like victims of a natural disaster, because we all have had one or two "wrecks." That's what we call it when your dog stops listening and chases the sheep around the field—or, worse, into the neighbor's cornfield. I knew that the clinic participants would believe me when I said that I needed help to avoid trouble. Everyone who works a sheepdog has been humbled when things don't go smoothly. ("Trouble" is not theoretical. Several sheep were lost in a cornfield during one trial, and two were never seen again. Months later, one turned up in the courtyard of an apartment complex miles away. Members of this breed of sheep, Barbados, look like antelope, which is why officials were called in to capture what looked like an escaped zoo animal.)

At first I walked Willie onto the field on-leash, asking everyone to keep their dogs away from him. I took deep breaths to stay calm. What if the disaster that my brain was always prepared for actually happened—in this context, a dogfight? But everything went well: Willie focused on the sheep, and the other dogs stayed away. Gradually, I let Willie spend more time in the presence of the other dogs, and on the second day, he met a big, mellow border collie named Vic.

I'd helped innumerable clients through the first introductions of dogs who used to be aggressive, often with my own stable of benevolent dogs. Keep your body loose. Breathe deeply and regularly. Don't stare, and don't loom over the dogs. I followed my own instructions, and everything happened just as it should. Willie was a bit tense, but Vic paid no attention and channeled Zenlike calm while I forced myself to let them alone. The dogs sniffed butts, acknowledged each other, and parted to scent-mark in the grass nearby. After a few seconds, I called Willie away and took him on a little walk. *Whew.*

I was ecstatic. It felt miraculous to watch Willie greet another dog without an incident after keeping him away from all but his close circle of friends for so long. As the day went on, Willie met other dogs, although only ones I had vetted by watching them greet other dogs. There were a few stiff-tailed males I decided to keep Willie away from, but most of the dogs at the clinic were relaxed and polite. Willie and I drove home at the end of the second day tired and happy, the green hills of Wisconsin rolling like swells of the ocean around us.

Willie continued to improve around other dogs as I sought out safe situations in which he could greet friendly dogs. Within a few months, he was able to walk into a vet clinic without exploding at some hapless beagle in the corner. After careful introductions, he made some new friends, and they'd romp and play in the orchard pasture, eyes shining, tongues lolling, as they ran shoulder to shoulder, stretching out like racehorses in big looping circles.

Willie's other problems improved at the same time. He didn't panic if a truck backfired going by the house. I'd found a diet that prevented his intestinal upsets. His fear of tall men was morphing into happy anticipation of a game of fetch. He never barked or growled when he spotted an approaching dog. He walked side by side with poodles and Pekingese with nary a nervous glance.

One night, after weeks of successful sessions with other dogs, I took Willie to meet a young border collie named Zip. The introduction went just as I'd hoped. Zip was passive and polite, and although Will was a bit stiff-legged during their greeting, he soon relaxed and the two began to do what all young social male mammals do: play. Within less than a minute, the two dogs were lost in a rousing game of chase.

Owners of reactive dogs or dogs who are aggressive to other dogs carry a unique kind of fear every time they walk their dogs. *Am I going to be leashed to a barking, snarling maniac if surprised by a dog around the corner? Will I be walking down the street and look up to see two large off-leash dogs barreling toward us, the owner a block behind them and waving at us with an oblivious grin, calling, "It's okay! They LOVE other dogs"?* Walking a dog who is afraid and/or aggressive to other dogs makes excursions outside at best anxiety-provoking and at worst a nightmare.

But Willie and Zip ran through the tall grass like buddies on a playground. They played "who can run faster" and "I've got the toy and you don't" while the sun dimmed behind the trees and the crickets played percussion in the background. Surely there is little more beautiful than two healthy young dogs bounding together across the grass.

Zip's owner also had a female boxer, Tango, who she said was good with other dogs. Unlike Zip, Tango was an adult female who wouldn't passively lie down to be inspected by a bumbling adolescent. She was muscled up like a wrestler and conveyed a sense of strength and confidence. Meeting her would be a good experience for Willie, because not all dogs he'd meet in the future were going to give him the upper hand during a greeting. Letting them meet was a small but reasonable risk, given that Tango was said to have good social skills and Willie was doing so well. The owner and I talked it out, and we decided to go ahead. Even as we spoke, however, a little voice inside asked me if we should proceed. Deep in my gut, a red flag was waving, but I ignored my intuition and decided to let the dogs greet each other.

Tango stood her ground as Willie approached, her legs straight, her head straining forward, neck flexed like a stallion's. The appropriate response of a young dog to an older, on-territory female would be to adopt an appeasing posture by lowering himself to the ground. But Willie responded by rearing up like a horse, attempting a "stand-over" by resting his forelegs on her shoulders. This is usually an active attempt by a dog to gain control of the interaction. A stand-over is not a wise move for an adolescent dog on an older female of a breed famous for never backing down. Worse, he growled at her. And then all hell broke loose when Tango growled back and lunged at Willie.

Imagine a blur of black and white streaking in erratic circles around the grass, followed by a growling mass of muscle. Every twenty strides, Tango would catch up to Willie and mash him into the ground with her forepaws and body, growling into his belly while Willie flailed and screamed. Tango's owner and I chased after the dogs in a frenzy, attempting to catch animals who were a gazillion times faster than we were.

Finally, we managed to get a hand on each of them. It probably took only a few seconds, but I remember the incident as if it lasted forever. As chaotic as things were, it was clear that Tango had not physically injured Willie. She'd simply told him in no uncertain terms that if anyone was going to do the growling, it was her. His panicked, high-pitched reaction had only aroused her more.

After the dogs calmed down, I did some work with Willie to end our visit on a good note, but what I remember most are the expletives I repeated as I drove home. This was exactly what I didn't want to happen; I knew it could set back Willie's progress considerably. Sure enough, the next time he saw an unfamiliar dog, Willie's reaction regressed into stiff-bodied growling and obsessive sniffing of urine marks.

Setbacks are common in treatment plans, no matter who you are or how much you know. "Stuff" happens less often if you have experience, but it still happens. Knowing this theoretically is one thing, but dealing with it personally is another. It takes more than knowledge to work on a serious behavioral problem. It also takes faith that it will work and, most important, the energy required to work through it day after day after day. I had the first two nailed. The third was a struggle.

I took a breath and wrote out a new treatment plan. Willie and I went back to basics yet again. We did hundreds of repetitions of the "watch" game. I reinforced good behavior both with tug games and by backing up a few steps to teach Willie that a calm response to another dog results in more distance, and thus less tension, between them. I asked little of Willie at first, keeping well away from dogs we saw on the street. I took him back to our local park that allowed dogs, sat in the car, and said "Watch" every time he spotted a dog. I took him to an empty dog training center and let him inhale the scents of other dogs until his nose was weary, then asked for watches rewarded by tug-of-war games. I enrolled in an outdoor training class that allowed us to stay on the other side of the fence, away from dogs, and we played the watch game over and over; I eventually letting Willie go up to the fence and sniff noses with dogs who seemed sweet and deferential.

After a month of this, Willie had progressed back to responding to approaching dogs with a loose body and a goofy grin. He continued to play keep-away with Sydney in the crusty snow on the high pasture, and he walked with Ashby as she hunted for field mice. And then his friend Zip, the border collie he'd played with so well just a month before, came to visit.

When Zip and his owner drove up, it was unusually quiet. Not a bird sang as I left the house with Willie. As expected, Willie automatically looked at me when he saw Zip, anticipating the good things he had learned to associate with other dogs. As we got closer, Willie continued to look relaxed, as if he'd love nothing more than to play with Zip. So I dropped the leash and let Willie run over to Zip. Everything looked good at first, Willie noodling over to Zip with his mouth relaxed and his body loose. Zip bowed down with a submissive grin on his face while Willie stood over him sniffing.

Just as I was about to lead the dogs to a play area, Willie attacked.

He lunged with an unmistakable look of pure, unmitigated rage and leaped on top of Zip, who squealed and threw himself to the ground. Willie's growls pierced the air. I never saw Willie's mouth attached to Zip; it was always open, teeth bared, eyes enraged. We got them separated soon enough, and it didn't appear that Zip had been hurt. But he was frightened.

So was I. The look on Willie's face as he attacked Zip was chilling.

People often object to the suggestion that dogs can feel the equivalent of human anger. "I'm shocked that you are engaging in such blatant anthropomorphizing," I was once told by a veterinary behaviorist after a speech I gave at the National Institutes of Health. Shaking with what appeared to be her own anger while the audience sat in stunned silence, she publicly castigated me for mentioning the words "anger" and "dog" in the same sentence.

And yet anger is a primitive emotion, as primitive as fear, and closely related to it. The neurobiologist John Ratey labels anger as the "second universal emotion," the first being fear. Not only are anger and fear universal in mammals, they can be hard to discriminate between. In people, ponies, and pandas, anger is the emotion that allows an individual to move past fear and take action to save itself, to protect its young, or to save its mate.

Most animal behavior scientists and animal trainers don't hesitate to talk about anger in mammals. Chimpanzee researchers, pig farmers, and dolphin experts often speak of an individual animal "going into a rage," or how easily irritated one particular individual animal might be.

However, it is one thing to accept that a rampaging chimpanzee can experience an emotion akin to anger, but it's another thing to attribute it to a dog. In his famous soliloquy on the loyalty of dogs, John Hobhouse wrote that dogs embody "all the Virtues of Man without his Vices." Dogs are said to give us "unconditional love," to greet us with unmitigated joy when we arrive home, and to accept us unquestioningly, no matter how flawed we might be. How could such a paragon of virtue experience the red-eyed rage that plagues our own species?

This vision of dogs as vessels of pure love and affection is dear to our hearts, and most dogs are indeed docile and loving, ridiculously so in some cases, forgiving their owners for a litany of abuses. But that doesn't mean they are incapable of the emotion of anger. They are equipped with the same structures in the brain that mediate anger in humans, produce the same set of neurohormones that create the emotion, and have expressions on their faces similar to those of humans when they are angry. When he went after Zip, the anger in Willie's eyes replicated the look on his face when he was but a tiny puppy and went after Pippy over a piece of food on the kitchen floor.

As I thought about it, I realized that Willie's reaction was most likely because Zip smelled like the boxer Tango. Tango's scent, and the bad memories it brought back, were reasonable explanations for Willie's response. However, it was the extremity of Willie's behavior that was so worrisome. After a long period of time and a vast array of treatments, his outbursts had become rare, but when they happened, they seemed pathological. Willie's expression when he went after Zip was shocking. He wasn't just protecting what he wanted by going on offense; his eyes had that strange combination of ice and heat that is associated only with out-of-control rage. It was anger multiplied by ten. Where in heaven's name would a young dog develop that kind of emotional intensity?

· · · · ·

Later that night, I heard coyotes yip-howling far away. Tulip heard them, too, and leaped up, barking low and loud at the front door, always quick to protect the flock from danger: "My sheep, my lambs, my land. Stay away!" She fretted for an hour, pacing and listening. I got up with her, moved to the couch, turned the television on and off. In spite of all of our progress, Willie still had a serious behavioral problem. Like Tulip, I couldn't settle down, filled with worry about Willie. While Tulip paced, I tore at my cuticles and scratched my mosquito bites.

As I worried, it occurred to me that Willie was acting like a dog with PTSD. Given my own symptoms, you'd think I would have figured it out sooner.

# CHAPTER TWENTY

When I was eighteen, I fell in love with Doug McConnell, a ruggedly handsome environmental activist whom I had met through my sister Liza. He swept me off my feet in about five minutes. We dated and married, and after seven years of living in different parts of the lower forty-eight, we wound up living in Ketchikan, Alaska, where Doug had gotten a job with the borough's planning department. This was before the oil pipeline, when Ketchikan was a soggy little town with endless rain, a lot of bars, one small grocery store with moldy apples and pitted potatoes, more bars, two restaurants, a bank, and a few tourist shops. It served the men who worked for long stretches in logging camps, on salmon fishing boats, and in the coast guard, and who got highly prized trips to town every so often. There were a lot of bars—did I mention that?

When the sun came out, it was glorious. Standing on the shore watching the sun sparkle off the sea, I saw a pod of orcas swim down the coast, massive black-and-white ovals curving through the water. At moments like those, I thought I was living in the most beautiful place on earth.

I got a job as a counselor for troubled adolescents, with a

paltry two weeks of training. I loved it; I worked with bright young kids who needed only a positive place to put their energy and someone to listen to them. Of all the children, I most vividly remember Marta: a raven-haired Native American who came into our program infamous as the town's best knife fighter. I would lean forward into her energy as she spoke, intensity radiating from her face, to listen to her voice, let her say what she had to say. A few years later, she successfully redirected her energy and was herself an administrator of a nonprofit agency that helped wayward teens.

In spite of the good days in Ketchikan, the oppressive, wet weather didn't make life in a moldy one-room cabin any easier. Nor did it help a marriage that just wasn't working. After two years in Ketchikan, I flew away from both the town and the marriage. At the airport, a suitcase in one hand and in the other a flat-faced Persian cat named Chat crammed into a travel case, I stood motionless beside Doug at the loading gate. Both of us looked down, words stuck in our throat, as Chat the cat yowled in fury.

Chat and I were heading to Madison, Wisconsin, where I'd been happiest in all of Doug's and my travels. At the time, I had one goal and one goal only: to live in one place for five years. That was forty years ago. I'm still here.

* * * * *

On my way back from Alaska, I was twenty-seven and reeling with the necessity of striking out on my own. Between flights at the Minneapolis airport, I met a blond, dapper guy in a designer suit and a Rolex. He wasn't my type. The only clothing labels I was familiar with had letters instead of names, like L.L.Bean and REI. To me, "sexy" is an outdoorsy guy in a flannel shirt and muddy boots.

Jason (as I'll call him) caught my eye while I waited at the gate for the next flight to Madison. He was tall and groomed like a GQ model, with perfect manicured nails and green eyes that drank me in like crème de menthe. Casual pleasantries led to conversation, which led to a drink at the bar. I don't drink much now—one drink is enough to make me slaphappy—but I barely drank at all back then. Just being in the bar at the airport was enticing in a delicious "I can't believe I'm doing this" way. One gin and tonic later, I slipped his phone number into my purse.

We talked a lot on the phone over the next few months. Actually, Jason talked and I listened. He was in real estate and sold expensive properties in Mexico. He was funny and interesting, and he encouraged me to visit him in Minneapolis. I kept thinking about his eyes, and a few months later, I was back in the Minneapolis airport. Jason picked up my bag, resting his hand on the small of my back as we moved through the crowd. I stopped in the restroom and reapplied my lipstick. We walked to his SUV in the parking lot, and I remember thinking that the car didn't fit the businessman image.

His place was in a development at the edge of town, four apartments to a building. There were open fields on one side of the complex, with plumes of goldenrod and scruffy asters swaying in a light breeze. It was dusk when we arrived, and I didn't see a soul as we left the parking lot, entered the building, and walked up the stairs.

We entered into the living room, and directly on our right was the door to the bedroom. Standing at the entrance, I could see the bed, covered with a brown quilted spread and a bedside table. There was nothing on the table except a lamp. And a gun. It was black and shiny, and it overwhelmed everything else in the room.

"Do you always have a gun in your bedroom?" I asked. He told me yes, he did. And that it was loaded.

"Oh." A little voice inside my head began to whisper that this wasn't good. I ignored it.

We settled into the living room and had a drink. As I got up to change for dinner, there was a backfire from a car outside, a loud, guttural BLAM! I turned to find Jason facedown on the floor. "Sorry," he said as he rose from the carpet. He'd been in 'Nam, he told me, and had never quite gotten over reacting to loud noises.

*Poor Jason*, I thought, *panicking just because he heard a loud noise*. Magazine articles and television shows were just beginning to mention the condition called PTSD, explaining how exposure to trauma caused some returning vets to be excessively fearful and sometimes have anger management problems. *I wonder if Jason has it, too*. I was fresh out of a job in social services, and I still wanted to save the world. Egotistically, I thought that maybe I could help him.

At least that was the conscious conversation I conducted with myself. But there was another one spoken by the inner observer that taps you on the shoulder. It said: *Something is wrong here. You should go*.

I ignored it, in part because it was so inconvenient. Where would I go? How could I get home? I had no vehicle and was completely reliant upon Jason. I could simply tell him I was sorry, I'd changed my mind and needed to go home, or to stay in a hotel, or to call a cab. But that would be awkward. I didn't want to be rude to this man who had unselfishly served our country. *Stop being stupid*, I told myself. *He's articulate and funny. Besides, he needs help.*

Jason laughed as he dusted off his jacket. "Don't worry," he said. "I'm fine. Just a little jumpy sometimes." He smiled, his green eyes crinkling. "Let's go have some fun."

We had dinner at a quiet restaurant, where he rested his hand on mine atop the white tablecloth. His touch made me tingle. We went back to his apartment and walked into his bedroom together.

And there was the gun again, sitting cold and black on the table right next to the pillow. Again that voice inside me said, *Stop, don't do this!*—and again I told it to shut up. *He's a nice man. It's not his fault that loud noises scare him and that he still doesn't feel safe after spending years in a war zone. Obviously, that's why he keeps a gun by his bed.* Besides, things hadn't been going well before I left my husband, and it had been a long time since I'd been with a man. It was intoxicating to feel wanted again, to feel the heat of a man's desire radiating warmth and energy like fire in a woodstove.

Jason unbuttoned my blouse and nuzzled my neck. He kissed my belly and unzipped my pants. We sank into his bed and began to kiss. And then, suddenly, before I could process what was happening, he grabbed me by the shoulders and flipped me over onto my stomach. He didn't say anything, just held me by the back of my neck and forced my face into the pillow. I yelled, "No! NO! STOP IT!" He didn't answer, but his body was a bull-like mass of force and power.

He sodomized me for an endless period of time. The pain was worse than I had imagined pain could be. My screaming and struggling made him even more violent, and he began to growl, "Bitch. You f—g dirty little bitch." Every time I protested, his grip hardened and his words got uglier. I went mute. I stopped struggling, but my face was pushed so hard into the pillow that it became hard to breathe. It occurred to me that he might kill me. As his breathing intensified, I was able to turn my head and suck in some air. The movement caused him to squeeze my neck even harder. I stopped moving altogether.

Finally, when he was done with me, he fell comatose on the pillow next to me. I lay frozen in bed beside him. I did not try to get up or call the police. I lay immobile the entire night, as if unable to move ever again, while he snored into the daylight. The fact that I lay there all night long makes no sense to me now. Why didn't I get up? Why didn't I call the police? Perhaps it felt safer to stay immobile than to try to move. Perhaps I was back in my own bedroom, as I had been years before, paralyzed with fear as my sister's boyfriend molested me. Or stunned into silence when a man fell out of the air and died at my feet.

• • • • •

By silent mutual agreement, Jason took me to the airport the next morning. As soon as we pulled up to the curb, I grabbed my bag and ran out of the car. I got on the plane, opened up a novel, and began trying to pretend it had never happened.

Blood flowed from my body for a few days after I came home, but I ignored it. I was too ashamed to go to a doctor. It never occurred to me to call the police. In the mid-seventies, a rape was a violent attack by a knife-wielding stranger who leaped out of the bushes. I had gone voluntarily into Jason's apartment, into his bedroom. There was no question in my mind that what had happened was my fault, just like being molested as an adolescent must have been my responsibility. Overwhelmed with the shame of it all, I told no one what happened in Minneapolis, not even my best girlfriend. I read a lot of mystery novels and willed myself to forget about it.

# CHAPTER TWENTY-ONE

I wasn't able to forget what had happened in Minneapolis, but I didn't talk about it. I tried once to tell a girlfriend but found that my throat tightened too much to get out the words. *Rape.* Such a horrible word. I couldn't say it aloud. And besides, it wasn't really a rape, was it? It was just the result of a stupid decision on my part, one that ended badly.

Along with the molestation and the trauma of watching Albert McCarthy die at my feet, the effects of the rape sat inside me, like a tiny tumor too small to see on an ultrasound. But I soldiered on, as we often do, willing myself to forget about it. I concentrated on my job, my studies, and my friends. Eventually, there were a lot of things that helped me excise it, but dogs played a leading role in my recovery.

My second husband, Patrick, and I bought my first border collie in the early eighties. His name was Drift. I met him when he was two years old, lying on a bed of straw in a barn straight out of a Wisconsin tourism calendar. Drift had a feathery black coat with a white fur collar as bright as a TV star's teeth, and a long sweeping tail that thumped against the weathered wood as I approached. I wanted to buy him after just one glance. I'd been in love with border collies ever since I'd first watched them herd sheep. It still seemed impossible that these beautiful dogs could dash away from one's feet, run two, four, six hundreds yards away in a sweeping semicircle, and ever so carefully nurse the flock toward you. Their combination of speed, power, and intelligence took my breath away. "Three-dimensional chess on fast forward," I called it. I'd never seen anything so exciting. I couldn't imagine living without a sheepdog a moment longer. Only problem was, we lived in a rental house and didn't have any room for sheep. No problem, I'd figure it out.

Jack took Drift out and worked him on a small flock of sheep, remarking that he'd had less training than usual for his age. I didn't have enough experience to evaluate his ability, but Drift's working potential wasn't really relevant at that point. He could have put his head on his paws and yawned at the sheep, for all I cared. I was smitten, flushed with dopamine-driven energy like My Fair Lady after the ball. I wanted this dog as much as I'd wanted anything in my life. I think his selling price was six or eight hundred, which at the time seemed an outrageous amount of money to pay for a dog.

Patrick may have loved dogs as much as I did, but he was appalled at the amount of money it would cost to bring Drift home. As we stood behind the barn, white sheep polka-dotting the green hills beyond, I said ridiculous things to try to convince him to spend the money. I promised that I would have a garage sale or eat beans for months. He took another look at Drift's grinning face and agreed we could take him home.

I spent Drift's first months with us in a haze of infatuation, enamored of every move he made. I'd catch myself staring at him while he slept, watching his chest rise and fall. I was riveted by everything about him, from the way he groomed himself like a cat to the way his ears pricked up at the base and flopped over at the tip. All he had to do was cock his head when I spoke and I'd melt for the twentieth time that day.

It wasn't all smooth sailing: He didn't eat for days, until I realized he was afraid to eat in my presence. He barked demandingly and had a stubborn streak more common in a coonhound than a border collie. But he was mine, he was brilliant, and he was beautiful.

Eventually, we found a farm to buy, and Drift and I got to work our own small flock of sheep. One late-summer day, Drift and I were working sheep in the big pasture high on the hill. The air was warm and heavy. Dark clouds were gathering to the south as I sent Drift to gather the sheep. A good border collie will stand motionless at your side until you give the cue to begin, at which point he'll explode into a ground-devouring run. Drift darted away as soon as I whispered, "Come Bye," the cue to run clockwise around the sheep. As he did, a Z of lightning split the sky; immediately afterward a crack of thunder shot through the valley. Drift seemed to ignore it and continued running around the sheep. By the time he'd gathered the flock, the sky looked even more threatening, and it had begun to rain. I said, "That'll do," and we retreated to the farmhouse, soaked to the skin.

A few days later, Drift and I went back up the hill to work sheep. As usual, he stood by my side, waiting for a quiet word to run in a semicircle around to the back of the sheep. I whispered, "Come Bye," but this time Drift stood immobile. I looked down at him in surprise. He turned his head away from me, looking toward the woods and the farmhouse. I moved a few feet to "reset" him and sent him again. He took the signal this time and did a nice outrun. Was it slower than usual? Perhaps. But once he got behind the sheep, he worked beautifully, enthusiastically, and we had a good session before it was time to let the flock rest. By the time we walked away from the flock, I had forgotten about his brief hesitation.

The next day, Drift and I were back up the hill. Again I settled him on my left side and said, "Come Bye." Drift moved forward, but instead of streaking toward the sheep in a wide semicircle, he began to trot toward the house. Astounded, I stood stock-still for a few seconds as I watched him move determinedly down the steep hill away from me and the flock. He loved working sheep, seemed to live for it, and always ran to them with an abundance of enthusiasm. But this time he might as well have said, "I quit," and walked away without looking back.

It made no sense to me at all. I called his name once, then again with more force. He put his head down and sped up, disappearing behind a wall of tree trunks and leaves. I followed silently, sure this time that something was terribly wrong. Once in the house he seemed fine, and when I took him to my veterinarian, he could find no sign of pain or illness. I called several trainers to find out how common it was for a dog to just walk off the job, and what they thought I should do about it. Several said that Drift should be punished for disobeying and I was spoiling him by letting him leave the sheep. But by then I knew enough about dog behavior to understand that what he had done had nothing to do with "dominance" or control. Drift was afraid of something, and he was telling me in the only way he knew how.

Because of the way I've told the story, no doubt the connection between Drift's behavior and the storm is apparent. However, for me, the time between the thunder and Drift's response was separated by a thousand other events. It didn't occur to me to associate the storm with his refusal to run to the sheep because, except for a brief pause, he'd behaved beautifully the first time after the thunder's boom. But months later, when a client came into my office with a dog named Barney, the wheels began to turn, and I made the connection.

Barney was your basic black Labrador, a big goofy horse of a dog who slap-danced into the room with his tail smashing into the walls and his torso careening into my legs. Aggression to strangers was clearly not the problem, but there *was* a problem—a big one. Though Barney had been going to dog parks for years, lately, he'd become an unwelcome guest. Barney had begun to pick fights with other dogs. They'd started out as minor skirmishes and had escalated into full-fledged battles.

Even worse, Barney was barking aggressively at dogs he saw while walking on a leash. The owners' once relaxing strolls through tree-lined streets had become tense, anxious ordeals. That was what had motivated Kathleen and Joshua to come to the office; they'd begun to avoid evening walks and had eliminated excursions to the dog park altogether. They knew that Barney needed more exercise than he was getting, and they wanted their happy, trustworthy dog back.

As we discussed the progression of Barney's behavior, his owners remembered that a few months ago he'd had a bad experience at the park. A large dog, new to the park, had threatened Barney when he dared to venture close to the dog's ball. The newcomer's stiff posture and quiet growl quickly escalated into an attack. As the dog bit at Barney's neck, the owners intervened and separated the dogs.

Barney had no visible injuries and seemed to shake it off. He appeared to be his usual joyful self at home. His owners noted nothing special about his next visit to the dog park. But on the subsequent trip, Barney reacted with a growl when another dog came up to greet him, and on the next trip, Barney began to charge at other dogs himself. Because Barney had seemed fine right after being attacked, and had behaved appropriately the first time he returned to the park, Kathleen and Joshua hadn't linked the attack and his behavior.

"That's right! Remember?" said Joshua. "He was attacked just a week before he began to growl at the dog park!"

Bingo. I immediately thought of Drift and the time he quit working sheep. It's amazing how the mind can hold facts adjacent, oblivious to their connection, until some miracle of neurons and electricity links them together. I'd seen that same pattern over and over in dogs just like Drift and Barney, who had been through some kind of frightening event and appeared fine at first but gradually evolved into being overly reactive to things that they had ignored in the past.

. . . . .

At the time, in the early nineties, I'd heard about PTSD, and even wondered if Jason suffered from it, but I didn't know much about it. Drift and Barney got me curious, so I began to do some reading. Although our understanding of the condition has increased exponentially over the years, and the details of the diagnostic criteria are in flux, the basics of PTSD haven't changed and are now well known to most of the public. After a traumatic event, some individuals develop a suite of persistent symptoms that include "increased physiological arousal" (difficulty sleeping, being easily startled or frightened, being easily irritated or angered), "avoidance or emotional numbing" (fearful reactions to previously positive or neutral events, trouble concentrating, avoidance), and "intrusive memories" (flashbacks or night-mares). Sometimes the symptoms show up right away, but often they are delayed for months or years.

At first I read about PTSD as a behaviorist, curious if this phenomenon might occur in dogs. The delay of visible reactions in people was especially interesting, since I had seen the same phenomenon in some of my clients' dogs. Like Barney, most of these dogs had been attacked by others at a dog park or on neighborhood walks. They behaved normally at first but were described as "completely different dogs" within a few weeks or months. Other dogs had been in car accidents or survived house fires. In every case, some kind of trauma had prefaced their change in behavior.

However, although we know that dogs can suffer emotionally, it isn't clear if they can experience the exact equivalent of PTSD in humans. So much of our understanding of PTSD is based on internal experiences described through speech, and even that is often inadequate. Even with humans' linguistic skills, people can go for years not knowing that what they are experiencing is related to an earlier trauma.

I should know. The man with the baseball bat appeared soon after the electrician fell to his death in Phoenix. However, I never made the connection between the fear and the trauma until I began therapy decades later. For decades, I had attributed my fear of being alone at night to a character flaw—a sign that I was inherently weak. By then, talking to therapists had allowed me to understand that being raped had filled me with shame and fear, and had added to the shock of seeing a man die at my feet.

Dogs, however, can't talk to therapists or write in journals about having nightmares, flashbacks, and trouble concentrating.

But there is no doubt that dogs are capable of being psychologically traumatized and suffering from some PTSD-related symptoms. One symptom is "hyperarousal," or a state of always being in fight-or-flight mode, just like Willie and me. The body becomes continually primed for danger, always on alert. We humans may be aware of a traumatic event in the past and talk about our flashbacks or nightmares, but the primary driving force of PTSD resides in the unconscious.

People who suffer from PTSD have systems that are out of balance—too much "on" and not enough "off." The brain is stuck in panic mode and perceives the world to be a relentlessly dangerous place. Minor events can elicit a response disproportionate to any potential danger. None of this is conscious, and none of this requires any kind of cognitive control that is beyond the ability of a dog.

Just as humans react differently to similar experiences, some dogs seem affected by trauma while others don't. I've evaluated dogs from horrific situations that might have psychologically crippled them for life, but they love their new homes and everyone they meet and sleep like puppies and go through the rest of their lives with silly grins and bodies loose and relaxed.

Other dogs appear to suffer terribly after a potentially traumatic event. I'll never forget hearing about a hollow-eyed dog who had been rescued just before death, having been abandoned among other dogs with no food, no water, and no means of escape. The dog watched his packmates die slowly and horribly of thirst and hunger, some cannibalizing the others in a desperate attempt to stay alive. He had come out of it as stunned as a soldier who had seen the worst of warfare, and it took months for him to learn that life could be safe and full of love and care, for him to do more than stare blank-faced out the window.

. . . . .

Drift and Barney were resilient and able to recover from their fears once we realized what had frightened them. Figuring that out was the key to changing their behavior. It was equally important for me to acknowledge that being raped had changed me forever.

My first therapist, Anne, helped me see that, yes, of course what happened in Minneapolis had been a rape. For years, when I allowed myself to think about it at all, I denied that it had been all that bad. I may have been afraid for my life, but Jason never threatened to kill me. I'd been injured, but I recovered physically within a week. It was far harder to recover from blaming myself for what had happened. I was on a date. I willingly went back to Jason's apartment. I willingly got in bed with him. How could that be rape? Anne helped me understand that it was: I had been silently threatened by the gun beside the bed, physically overpowered, and violently assaulted.

I also worked through the aftermath of rape by reading more about it. I began a book titled *After Silence* by Nancy Venable Raine, but after reading for ten minutes I literally threw the book away from me. It landed on the floor, pages creased, cover bent. I didn't feel better after beginning the book; instead, I felt worse.

Nancy had been unpacking boxes in the kitchen of her new apartment when a stranger broke in and, for hours on end, raped her repeatedly at knifepoint, telling her he was going to kill her. What had happened to her was so horrific that I was overwhelmed not just with sympathy for her but with disgust for myself. How could I equate her experience with mine? Ridiculous. Here I had come to the realization over the years that what happened with the Vietnam veteran had indeed been rape, but obviously, I was just coddling myself. What had happened to *her* was rape. What had happened to me was a bad date.

It took weeks before I could pick the book up again. Doing so was one of the best decisions I've ever made. Somehow, partway through, I began to forgive myself for being traumatized by what had happened to me. Instead of defining it as "not bad enough," I began to see the universals in one's responses to being raped, and to understand why I had said so little about it. There's a perfect storm of reasons why rape victims are silenced, both by themselves and by others.

For one thing, talking about sexual assault is a form of exposing yourself. We're talking about the areas of your body that you protect from others—your "private parts." The definition of "private" is: "secluded from the sight, presence, or intrusion of others." No surprise then, that when you are assaulted in areas so personal they act to define your perception of self, you don't want to compound the violation by talking about it.

Another reason that victims don't talk about sexual assault or other horrific traumas is that we simply can't explain the consequences. Nancy Venable Raine sums this up in a sentence that took my breath away: "The loss of a sense of safety is impossible to imagine when you still possess it, and nearly impossible to regain once you have lost it." How do you describe to someone what it's like to live with the knowledge that at any instant you will be attacked from the inside out?

Being internally attacked is such a unique and horrific

experience that I don't think it's possible to imagine it if it hasn't happened to you. Perhaps that's part of why some traumas are so isolating; why soldiers don't want to talk about what they went through when they come home, why rape victims turn in to themselves and go silent. It is part of why I never wanted to talk about what had happened. I felt as though language could not explain a phenomenon so primal that it is beyond words. After the rape, it seemed as though I had been hollowed out, with my sense of self gone, and nothing left with which to replace it.

When I finally was able to begin talking about it, I told a friend that it was like trying to function as a person without skin, with muscles and nerve fibers naked and exposed.

The worst result of the rape was the loss of my ability to speak even to myself about it. As Judith Herman says in *Trauma and Recovery*, "Certain violations of the social compact are too terrible to utter aloud: this is the meaning of the word *unspeakable*." No wonder I was so busy . . . busy avoiding thinking about something too awful to contemplate. This is the most profound crime of rape—it not only isolates you from others, it isolates you from yourself. As Nancy Venable Raine says, while others focus on the sexual aspect of a rape, in real life its primary victim is one's "memory and identity."

· · · · ·

Facing all three events—being molested, watching a man fall through the air and die at my feet, and being raped a decade later—was the first step in my recovery. Gradually, I began to realize that much of my behavior—which I had ignored or explained to myself as "character flaws"—was based on events in my past that I had willed myself to forget. Sensing a man about to kill me is a classic type of flashback for people who have experienced a traumatic fright. I might have not been particularly brave as a young child, but my terror of being alone at night after being molested and seeing a man die was far beyond that of a five-year-old frightened by a horror movie.

As hard as it was—and make no mistake about it, it was awful at first—to face the traumas that had shaped my life, I never could have moved on if I hadn't done so.

· · · · ·

Willie, on the other hand, had no event that would explain his behavior—at least not that anyone knew about. What was clear was that he had a lot to worry about. To him, the world was a dangerous place. Unfamiliar dogs were especially scary. Unexpected noises were harbingers of great danger. Much of the time, life was glorious, full of new people ("Look! There's another one!") and the languorous joy of grinding his shoulder into a pile of fox poop. But he had to be ever alert for danger. Fear and its partner, anger, were always present, like the sight of a flock of ephemeral sheep, fading in and out behind the trees.

That was my Willie, even as an eight-week old puppy. Could a dog that young have experienced a trauma so horrific that it changed the very nature of his brain? What had happened when he was alone in the litter; what frightening event might have traumatized him so severely that his very nature was changed? Or was he just wired differently than normal? Did he arrive at birth as a squalling wet sock of a puppy already programmed genetically to be on high alert? We don't know what particular genetic blueprint could have sent him into the world with a brain functioning like that of a combat survivor.

No matter what the cause, he behaved as though he had been psychologically traumatized. My heart broke for him every time he exploded off the carpet, startling to the quietest of sounds. The only problem was, I did, too. No wonder we were soul mates.

# CHAPTER TWENTY-TWO

"Take one dog and call me in the morning" is not a prescription you will ever hear from your doctor, but it would be a reasonable one. Healthy, happy dogs can be good for us. The research is clear: The mere presence of a dog can elevate your levels of oxytocin, the hormone that makes you feel all warm and melty toward someone you love. Oxytocin can also decrease feelings of fear and anxiety. Shock and trauma are not just theoretical concepts; they affect your entire body, and they not only compromise brain function, they actually change the size of the areas of your brain that mediate emotion. Stroking a dog, or even just looking at one, can increase your levels of oxytocin and can be as therapeutic as taking a drug.

When Willie wasn't leaping up in terror of an unexpected noise or barking like a banshee at another dog, he was the best therapist one could imagine. The best of Willie was the best a dog could be—a dog who loved you as if you'd hung the moon or, perhaps more appropriately, as if you'd independently discovered food. Every day when I arrived home, he greeted me like a best friend he hadn't seen in years. He snuggled against me every evening, resting his chin in the dip between my neck and shoulder, pressing his face against my skin. I'd rest my palm against the plush of his fur, the silk of his belly, and my heart would calm like a lake's silver surface in the evening.

· · · · ·

One of my motivations to switch from studying primates to working with dogs was the need to touch the animals I was working with. I had loved observing the tamarins years before at the university, but the less they were handled, the better. We were studying their social behavior in as natural an environment as possible in the physical constraints of the building, and we needed to keep their relationships as natural as possible. But sometimes the adolescents would leap onto my shoulder when I was adding new branches into their cage or bringing them a new food dispenser to play with.

Zooey, a young adolescent male, liked to play with my earrings; he had an unfortunate tendency to try to pull them off, so I quickly learned to avoid wearing even the simplest of jewelry. But his favorite interaction was to peer into my mouth. He seemed fascinated by it—he'd sit on a branch at face height and peer down intently toward my lips. Once he used his paws to open my mouth and look inside, pulling up on my upper jaw with his left paw, pulling down on my lower jaw with his right. I had to discourage those interactions, but I always left the monkeys wanting to touch them, to stroke their silly, wiry heads of hair, to scratch their tiny little bellies.

As a canine behaviorist, I saw hundreds of dogs every year who begged to be petted. And pet them I did, thousands and thousands of them over the years, from the silky ears of Yorkshire terriers to the soft flat coat of rottweilers that smoothed over their muscled shoulders like a satin glove.

Of course, I couldn't pet them all. About 80 percent of my clients came in because their dogs were aggressive in some context; about half were aggressive to other dogs, half to people. Many of the dogs begged me with body language to stay away from them, voicelessly telling me how frightened they were, to please, please, give them some time to get to know me. A few others sauntered in and told me clearly and confidently to keep my hands to myself. Confident dogs such as those were rare, fear being by far the most common motivation behind snarling and biting, though there were a few who looked in my eyes like a hit man holding a .44 Magnum, and dared me to reach toward them. I didn't. Who said that dogs should submit to petting by anyone and everyone who feels like it? I learned to reassure the owners that I loved their dog, even if I wasn't petting him or her immediately. "Chomper is adorable! Look at that crazy tail! I'm not petting him now only because he is asking me not to. Do you see how he is turning his head away from me and flicking out his tongue? That's his way of telling us that he is nervous and needs some time to adjust before I try to pet him."

The irony did not escape me. I became a behaviorist in part because I wanted to be able to physically interact with animals rather than hiding in a blind and observing them from a distance. And here I was, working with a multitude of dogs who didn't want to be touched, at least not at first, not until I'd helped them get over their fears and learn to trust strangers. But I could give them a voice, and that felt even more important.

The irony also did not escape me that I had a dog at home who, depending on the moment, either helped me to heal or set me back. But as we worked through it together, gradually, week by week, month by month, Willie began to settle down.

I did so many things to try to help Willie that it is impossible to say what had the biggest impact. I spent hours every week planning and implementing conditioning sessions, during which Willie's limbic system—the primitive alarm system—rewired itself to associate approaching dogs with feeling playful and relaxed. Veterinarians with extensive training in herbal medicine and acupuncture treated him for his reactivity and nervousness every two weeks. I took Willie to my yoga master, Scott, and learned exercises designed to calm his reactive nervous system, since dogs' nervous systems are so similar to our own.

At the same time, I continued my own therapy, concentrating on my excessive startle response, an acknowledgment that the traumas in my past had reset my own physiology. I surrounded myself with soothing scents. I had sessions with the yoga master once or twice a month. I meditated, although never as much as I felt I should. I tried hard to eat good, healthy food that stabilized rather than amped me up. Sometimes I succeeded. I continued to write in my journal every morning, and for the first time, I began talking with a few others outside of therapy, people I knew well and trusted, about the things that had happened to me. I had told Jim some of what had happened to me years before, but now I gathered my courage to tell him the full story. He listened, kissed my hands, and gently swept my tears away with his fingers. In his work at a mental health institute, he'd seen many women who had suffered terribly from traumas in their past. "It is so important for you to work through this, Trisha," he said. "I'll do everything I can to be there for you while you do."

As I spoke to others in my circle of friends, I was stunned to discover how many had been sexually traumatized in some way. On the one hand, it was depressing that so many people I knew had experienced sexual violence. I knew how common it is for young people to be molested or raped, but statistics don't prepare you to sit across the table from someone you've known for years and learn the horrible things that had happened to her in her past.

But there was a good side to giving voice to the traumas of the past. I felt inspired by each woman who told me her story: Look what happened to her, and look how amazing she is now! I found myself feeling less alone as I listened to their stories. The isolation of trauma can bury you, underground and alone, like an injured cat hiding silently under the porch. Your intellect tells you to call out for help, but your emotional brain tells you to stay silent, that your only safe alternative is to hide, alone and mute, even if it means you'll never make it out. There are worse things than death.

Talking about trauma doesn't kill you, and as long as it is done in a safe environment, it turns out to be liberating instead of dangerous. It is not always easy. In some ways, it's like working out at a gym: Afterward your muscles might be sore, but you know it's constructive in the long run. Along with the physical work I was doing—diet, yoga, meditating—talking about what had happened took away some of its power.

Talking, however, can only go so far, so I spent a lot of time trying to repair my internal physiology. I cuddled with Jim, hugged friends, and got massages. I petted my dogs, stroking their soft cheeks, their satiny pink bellies, and let oxytocin, my "drug" of choice, do its work.

· · · · ·

One evening a few birds sounded off with a chirp as they settled in their nightly roosts. I listened to hear whether the barred owl would call: "Who cooks for YOU? Who cooks for YOU?" Not tonight, I guessed; the sky turned navy blue and the light from the barn turned a thick buttery yellow while the trill of the snowy tree crickets joined the buzz of the cicadas as all the birds cozied in to sleep.

I pulled the shades and lay down on the living room carpet, the light of a lamp from my mother the only brightness in the room. Willie lay down beside me, his head resting on my shoulder, his long body stretched out beside mine. Lassie cuddled against my other flank, her ribs rising and falling with each breath. Tulip was curled up at my feet, which nestled underneath her fur.

On this night, Willie was calm, and every so often he exhaled a little louder, with a soft moan deep from behind his throat. I made a little humming noise in return. He pushed his head farther into the crook of my neck, and I rested my right hand in the velvet of his belly. Just me and the dogs, taking our medicine.

# CHAPTER TWENTY-THREE

The summer's heat was brutal, and I was happy to be sitting cross-legged in the cool of the downstairs bathroom. Inside the small windowless room, I could hear the babbling of baby wrens drifting from the vent that was supposed to funnel humid air out of the room. Years ago a family of house wrens had taken over the vent as a perfect nesting site. The first year, when I turned on the fan, the babies would chitter in complaint. I imagined them like tiny pilots in open cockpits with their sparse feathers flying sideways, Snoopy-like, in the breeze. Then the fan stopped working, and I bequeathed the vent to the wrens in perpetuity.

I was also listening to the hissing of Brave, a five-week-old kitten whom I had trapped a few hours before in the barn. He and his four littermates appeared two weeks earlier at the edge of the haymow. At first all I saw was a furry orange tail disappearing down a hole. The next day, a tiny face emerged and then darted back into the darkness. As the days went on, it became clear that a feral cat had delivered her litter in my barn, and that the little ginger kitten had four brothers and sisters.

I caught glimpses of Mom, a petite black-and-orange tortoiseshell, as she darted out of the barn and disappeared into the undergrowth. She was shy and wary, and the few times she saw me, she reacted as if her life depended on getting away. It well might have; some people in the country call cats "ditch rats" and enjoy shooting them. Her kittens were equally frightened, in spite of my sitting day after day beside their play area, tossing them food, being careful not to chase or frighten them more than they already were. Over a period of weeks, I conditioned them to go into a dog crate for pieces of chicken that I'd toss inside, while I sat sweating twenty feet away in ninety-five-degree weather. Finally, when they seemed old enough to be away from their mother and at risk of being taken by a fox or a hawk, I held my breath and pulled the string, slamming the crate door shut. They yowled in terror while I carried them inside, and they ran to huddle behind the toilet when I released them into the bathroom.

Few animals express fear better than a frightened kitten. With eyes seemingly too big to fit inside their heads, they paste their ears to their skull and gape their mouths open in a threatening hiss. I named the hissy boy Brave, the name of the Pixar movie about a Scottish lass with a ridiculous mane of red hair and an equal amount of moxie. I considered retracting the name, given that he seemed the most fearful of all, but I kept it, realizing that of all the kittens, he was the one most willing to face his fears.

Our own fears aren't always so simple or logical; nor do we often acknowledge or face them directly. Sometimes fear causes us to make illogical decisions, as when we avoid traveling in a foreign country that is much safer than our own but get into a truly dangerous situation—like being in a car—without giving it a second thought. We worry about a multitude of improbable events, from dying of a rare disease to being in an airplane crash.

And yet, as author Gavin de Becker describes in *The Gift of Fear*, while we are busy worrying about things that are unlikely to hurt us, we ignore and dismiss important signals of danger. These signals don't come from the media or government statistics. They come from deep inside of us; from our own private security system that is hard-wired into the most primitive parts of our brain. Something tells us, some little nagging voice deep inside, that there is danger. And often we ignore it.

That's exactly what I did when I was raped. "Don't be silly," I said to myself when my intuition began waving red flags. "He's a nice man." A nice man with a loaded gun in his bedroom and a violent and excessive reaction to a common noise.

After reading de Becker's book, I suspect there were other indicators that my safety had been compromised. However, although those clues may be objective and factual, we may not be consciously aware of them. De Becker tells the story of a man who walked into a convenience store and immediately left without buying anything because of an overwhelming sense of dread. The next person to enter was shot and killed. While being interviewed after the crime, the survivor said that he had no idea why he had left the store. But as he talked it out, he realized that he had actually noticed a group of signals that were full of information: Except for one brief, nervous glance, the clerk didn't greet him as usual; instead, he kept his gaze locked on another customer who was wearing a heavy jacket on a hot day. A car sat outside with the engine running.

"Now it's all clear," the survivor noted—the frightened clerk, a gun hidden under a coat, a getaway car in the parking lot—"but it didn't mean a thing to me at the time."

"Actually," said de Becker, "it did then, too." The survivor just added up all the facts unconsciously, in the part of his brain responsible for keeping him safe. And yet because we worship rational, conscious thought and demean what we call intuition, we often dismiss and ignore it. I am not the only woman who has said "Don't be silly" when her inner voice told her there was danger. In case after case noted by de Becker, women didn't listen to that little voice and were raped and/or almost murdered. Others aren't alive to talk about it.

As I went through the initial steps of facing my past, I learned that just listening is not enough. It's important to listen to and act on that little voice. Like many women, I may have heard what my body was telling me, but I let concerns about being embarrassed or hurting someone's feelings override it.

A few months after beginning work with my therapist, I was traveling and my back was killing me, so I scheduled a therapeutic massage at the hotel. I could just squeeze one in after speaking at a nearby bookstore and grabbing some sleep before an early wake-up call.

No one else was in the hotel spa except the masseur. The moment I entered the lobby, a quiet wave of anxiety swept through me. How does one describe that sensation, the feeling in your gut that both whispers and yells at the same time? It is so strong and yet so hard to specify, living as it does in the most primitive, nonverbal part of our bodies. These alerts to danger aren't only in our brains: We know now that we have a second nervous system, the enteric nervous system, which lives in our intestines and communicates with our brains on a moment-by-moment basis. No wonder we talk about "gut feelings." There are neurons in our intestines, the same cells that we have always called "brain cells," but our bellies contain no centers of speech and language, and thus we struggle to describe the feeling.

Before I began therapy, I would have dismissed the wave of

fear that lapped through me that night, using all the arguments de Becker has heard hundreds of times: "I thought I was just being silly," "I didn't want to cause a fuss," or "It would have been rude to leave." But this time I acted on it. I don't remember what I said, exactly, except that I handled it poorly. I stammered and apologized repeatedly, no doubt exhaustingly so. I suspect that when I finally backed my way out of the room, the man was relieved that I had gone.

When I relayed the incident to my therapist, she cheered and clapped. Rather than suggesting that I was being paranoid, she reinforced my behavior like a trainer giving a dog treats for a difficult recall. We had a little party in her office over it, and I have no doubt that is why, a few years later, I was able to prevent a situation that might have been far more serious.

In that case, the same indescribable feelings of being in danger arose in a completely different context. It was during the day, in my own office with other people just yards away, and yet I was overwhelmed with a sense that the man talking to me intended to harm me. He had come in upset about a neighbor's dog and the advice I had given the owners about how to handle the animal's behavioral problems. He wasn't yelling; he spoke in a low, quiet voice. At first his words were not threats; much of what he said was supposed to be complimentary. But as he talked, his smile never reached his eyes, and eventually, he moved to within inches of my face, and his eyes went flat and hard as he said, "I know how much you love your dogs. It'd be such a shame if something happened to them."

This time there were no internal arguments or rationalizing. I had no doubt that I could be in danger, not necessarily at that particular moment but in the future. Nor did I become paralyzed with fear, as I had so often in the past. I spent the next few weeks taking steps to protect myself and my dogs that still amaze me in their clarity of purpose. I avoided being alone; I reached out to friends who agreed to watch the house. I alerted the appropriate authorities. I learned a bit about self-defense. Nothing happened, but what matters is that I acted on my fears and morphed from defense to offense. I'd finally learned my lesson and qualified for the Olympics of taking care of myself. I knew it didn't mean I'd always get the gold, but at least now I had a chance.

· · · · ·

Willie learned to face his own fears, too. One day I needed him to push the sheep through a gate. They didn't want to go, not at all, being correct in the belief that once they did, they would be trapped, wormed, and vaccinated: the ovine equivalent of going to the dentist. By then, Willie had all the training he needed to get the job done. He knew cues for pushing the sheep forward, backing away from them if necessary, and moving clockwise and counterclockwise around them. He could run two hundred yards away from me and bring me the flock, speed up or slow down when asked, and drive sheep off the feeder pans so that I didn't get run over by the flock. As a young dog, he was already an invaluable farmhand. However, in this case I was asking him to do a very grown-up job.

One ewe in particular was the problem. Barbie was a pretty yearling when I adopted her as a favor to a friend. In spite of her small stature, she had matured into the flock's leader and senior enforcement officer. Barbie would tell you right away if your dog had what it took to work sheep. She did job interviews in an instant, correctly reading a dog's confidence, or lack of it, in one glance. At the slightest sign of hesitation, Barbie's head went down, her anvil-thick forehead facing the dog. Many a time she had smashed toward a dog, charging forward like some petite woolly bull.

As Willie learned to work the flock, I supported him by walking up behind him when Barbie challenged him. Barbie learned that she wasn't going to win, and Willie learned that he could back her down. Gradually, my presence was rarely necessary. But this time Willie was at the edge of his abilities, and I needed to stay by the gate to hold it open. I decided that Willie was old enough to step up to the challenge, so I asked him to face off Barbie on his own and force her inside the pen.

First Barbie tried an end run around Willie to the right, but like a World Cup soccer goalie, he cut her off. Another ewe tried to scramble past Willie on the left, practically leaping over him in the attempt. Willie cut her off, too. Time after time, the sheep attempted to dart away, zigging left or zagging right, and Willie blocked every attempt. But they wouldn't move forward through the gate, and although Willie was working hard, the sheep were only moving sideways.

It had been a long time since Willie had busted in on the sheep. He had never bitten, and in spite of his early attempts at lunging, he had been remarkably trustworthy around the flock. I love sheep, and I hate to see them scared or injured. But sometimes a working sheepdog has to use more than his presence to convince them. Although no good shepherd wants her sheep hurt, sometimes the woollies just have to learn that dogs have weapons inside their mouths and are willing to use them if necessary. Busting in on the sheep to bully them is one thing, but using your power to get the sheep moving is another. A quick nip on the nose can be appropriate if the dog has good bite inhibition, nips lightly, and lets go instantly. Not all dogs have the emotional control to do that. My little Misty, a powder puff with people, was so frightened of confrontations with sheep that she'd dart in, sink her teeth into a sheep's ear—always the left one—hanging on for dear life with her eyes squeezed shut in terror. Not good. But Willie had never used his mouth on the flock, in part because he was, pure and simple, a good dog. It was also because he was afraid of confronting the sheep. And Barbie knew it.

Back at the gate, Willie continued to block the flock's attempt to escape, but he began to spend more moments in a stiff-bodied face-off with Barbie. Finally, she turned and flat-out charged Willie, her head level with his, her hard, bony forehead poised to smash him into the ground. In a rare moment of wisdom, I kept my mouth shut. And instead of darting backward to avoid her, for the first time in his life, Willie met her head-on, lunging forward and nipping her nose. He let go right away, and for a second, everything went still.

Barbie stopped as if she'd received an electric shock. Willie stood his ground and stared straight into her eyes. A second later, she charged him again, and again he threw himself forward and, at just the right instant, nipped her nose. She stopped, backed up, and appeared to reappraise the situation. No one breathed. It was abnormally quiet, as if even the birds had stopped singing. And then Barbie turned her head, grudgingly walked into the pen, and the rest of the flock followed.

# CHAPTER TWENTY-FOUR

Aladdin, a lithe mixed-breed dog with long eyelashes and expressive eyes, came into my office because he had a bad habit: He lunged at people, seemingly randomly. His big brown body would charge at them, mouth open, teeth sharp and hyperwhite inside coal black lips. His owner, a young woman named Clara, looked as vulnerable as Aladdin looked strong. She dissolved in tears and melted into her chair as she told me about the times Aladdin had frightened her friends. Her eyes scrunched and swollen, she explained how much she loved her dog and couldn't imagine living without him.

And yet there were those lunges. All potential aggression from dogs should be taken seriously, but being lunged at by a large dog with jaws powerful enough to break your arm is especially hard to ignore. Clara had a time bomb on her hands, but Aladdin was the family she'd never had, and now everyone was telling her to put him down.

Aladdin hadn't read his rap sheet. Rather than entering the office on high alert, he padded up to me with his body relaxed and swaying. He bowed his head for neck rubs and then lay down comfortably between Clara and me. Clearly, his behavior had little to do with being afraid of strangers.

As I talked to Clara, I looked for a pattern in Aladdin's behavior. The more predictable a behavior problem, the more likely it can be solved. But Aladdin's lunges didn't seem to follow the usual format. He wasn't more likely to go after men than women or strangers rather than friends. He had even lunged at Clara one day when she came home from shopping. He'd lunged over the backseat and terrified a girlfriend when she entered the car. He'd charged after one deliveryman, but not one from the same company as the day before. His veterinarian had found no health problems that could explain his behavior.

I knew there had to be a reason for Aladdin's behavior, if only we could have asked him. Mostly, I think it's good that dogs can't talk; I'm not convinced that we'd always like what they have to say. However, their lack of voice makes it impossible for them to tell us what is wrong, to explain their behavior in ways that we can understand. All I could do was gather information, to look for some pattern that we had not yet identified.

In hopes of learning more, I suggested that we leave the office and go for a walk in a secluded area behind my office. I asked to take Aladdin's leash once we got outside, being as concerned about the safety of others as I was about Clara and Aladdin. It was chilly but sunny, so in preparation to go outside, I put on my jacket and sunglasses. Aladdin took one look at me and leaped up at my face.

He didn't bite me. For that matter, he'd never bitten anyone, and he'd had ample opportunity to do so. But he was scary, and the potential of serious injury loomed. I knew that we had to figure out what it was that set Aladdin off before someone got hurt.

After Aladdin lunged, I took off my sunglasses to talk about what had just happened. As soon as I did, Aladdin put his head down and shook his entire body, as dogs often do after being stressed, and flashed me a sloppy grin.

*Sunglasses.* That was the trigger that had set off Aladdin when Clara entered the house, when her girlfriend got in the car on a bright sunny day, and the difference between the deliverymen. Sunglasses off? Aladdin loved you. Sunglasses on? Aladdin responded as if you'd pulled a gun out of your pocket. In his mind, you had. Lots of dogs respond to sunglasses, which must appear to them as huge round eyes with dilated pupils. Eyes of that description are signs of trouble, and not just in a canine society. Butterflies, caterpillars, snakes, frogs, and even whales use false eyespots, circles much larger than their actual eyes, to startle predators or to confuse them. People interested in gaining or maintaining power often wear sunglasses, not just to conceal their eyes but also to enlarge them to look more formidable. Conjure up an image of a young military man in a country enmeshed in political turmoil, and looming behind the ubiquitous AK-47 will be a face punctuated by two large black circles staring at you, the lenses unwavering like a hard eye of a dog about to bite.

To Aladdin, I had morphed instantly from a relaxed, benevolent acquaintance into a highly aroused and potentially dangerous one. Aladdin was just going to get me first, before I could get him.

It was an ideal discovery, the information every behaviorist hopes for: a clear trigger that can be replicated safely during training. Sunglasses are a perfect fit for a treatment plan, because an owner can have complete control over when the dog is exposed to them. Clara began to wear them in the house while she was feeding or playing with Aladdin. We taught Aladdin that "sunglasses on" meant he got to play ball or eat chicken or get his belly rubbed. Friends came over and, with Aladdin safely behind a gate, began throwing treats to him immediately after putting on their glasses, then taking them off and withdrawing the treats.

This linking of "trigger" with "treat" is as effective with people as it is with dogs. You link a low-intensity version of the trigger (or "bad" thing) with a high-intensity version of a treat (the "good" thing), so that one's response to the treat becomes one's response to the trigger. This was the method I had been using to help Willie with other dogs and tall, unfamiliar men. It is the legacy of Pavlov and his own dogs, who taught us that one can transfer positive emotions to a neutral or negative event if done with the right timing and in the correct order.

While sunglasses were the trigger that elicited fear in Aladdin, it's not always so easy to figure out what scares a dog. Or a person. Until I began therapy, I never associated having a man fall "out of the blue" and die at my feet with the feeling that someone behind me was about to smash me in the head with a baseball bat. In some ways, those scenarios bore no relation to each other. But their essence—the part that was recorded in the most primitive part of my brain—could not have been more similar. Their message was: "At any moment, when you least expect it, something horrible and life-threatening is about to happen."

Sometimes the triggers that set someone off don't seem, at first glance, to make any sense. Nancy Venable Raine, the author of *After Silence*, began having flashbacks about her car falling from the Golden Gate Bridge after viewing scenes from an earthquake in Japan. Superficially, there are no connections between a horrific car accident, an earthquake, and being raped.

Neither are there obvious links between watching a man die and the sensation of being stalked by a bat-wielding psycho. But logic isn't always relevant when talking about a brain changed by trauma. What *is* logical is that once they learn to expect the worst, traumatized brains can be set off by a wide range of triggers. Part of healing is figuring out what they are.

· · · · ·

Aladdin's story ended happily. After a few months of perseverance by his owner, he paid little attention to sunglasses. He did still have one problematic behavior: On occasion he would forget his manners and run up to a stranger who was wearing sunglasses, but his intentions were now friendly, and his message was some doggy version of "Hello, HELLO! I see you have on those strange eye things. Could I please then have an order of chicken, or is it turkey that comes with sunglasses today?"

Aladdin taught me never to approach a dog I don't know while wearing sunglasses; I reflexively take them off when I see a new dog, and I always ask anyone beside me to do the same. My husband has probably heard "Jim, you'd better take your sunglasses off" more times than he cares to count, because he has helped with scores of reactive dog cases, and because sunglasses are a perfect example of a seemingly innocuous thing that can elicit dramatic responses in the brains of any mammal, including dogs and people. I should know—dramatic responses used to be my middle name.

· · · · ·

I was at the local airport not too many years ago, where I've been so often that I have a visceral reaction to Willie Nelson's song "On the Road Again." I've flown so many times that airports, the last place you'd think anyone would look to for solace, have a sense of comforting familiarity. But this time I was trembling with fear as I stood in the security line. I began deep breathing, trying to calm my pounding heart. My local airport had just installed the whole-body scanners in which you stand with feet spread apart and arms raised overhead while an image of your unclothed body is analyzed by a TSA agent. I'd been in them before, and each time I walked out shaking, sometimes on the verge of tears.

I can't say exactly why this one experience was such a powerful trigger. Was it that I had my hands over my head while I was being raped? Or was it just the generalized sense of being violated, of being told to spread your legs apart and hold your arms over your head, where you can't use them to protect yourself, while a stranger looks at your body? As is often true of traumatic triggers, it doesn't really matter all that much why it sets off the primal part of your brain that is screaming, "YOU ARE IN DANGER OF DYING"—it's just that it does.

As the line moved forward and the machine loomed closer, the woman behind me recognized me and said hello. I attempted to engage in casual conversation while hiding my shaking hands. At other times I had avoided the scanner and elected to be physically searched, but often that felt equally intrusive. Just seeing the scanner became almost as upsetting as going through it.

Finally, it was my turn. I must have been ashen-faced, because the agent, a strapping young man, couldn't hide his look of disdain. Condescendingly, he said, "It's really nothing."

"Not if you've been raped, it's not!" I snapped. I didn't plan to say it—the words darted out of my mouth like a frog's tongue after a fly. And I didn't say them quietly; everyone within twenty feet heard them. I'd been writing about being raped before this particular trip, and doing that must have given me the courage to say the word "rape" out loud instead of keeping it enclosed like some ugly, oozing wound hidden under a bandage. No one moved for the longest time. I had no idea what the acquaintance behind me was thinking; I never turned around to see her face.

The agent was immobilized after my comment, so I spoke more softly, saying something like "It might be helpful for you to understand that for some people, based on their experience, this is actually a very difficult thing to do." He nodded, still shocked, and I walked inside, spread my legs, and shook even harder than usual while I raised my arms over my head and tried to breathe.

After that trip, I realized I had to get a handle on my response to body scanners. I needed to use the same method I'd used on Aladdin for sunglasses and Willie for other dogs. I took a low-intensity version of something that scared me and had it lead to a high-intensity version of something I love.

Linking something scary with something good sounds simple, but this kind of conditioning is so powerful that it can cause problems if you don't do it right. Nancy Venable Raine covered a new apartment with the scent of roses and gardenias in order to associate it with beautiful things, and ended up conditioning herself to feel anxious any time she smelled those particular flowers.

The keys to making this work are timing (trigger first) and modulating the intensity. Intensity is the tricky part. The trigger has to be presented first at a high enough level to be perceived as relevant to the problem, but at a low enough intensity to avoid eliciting real fear. That is not always as easy as it sounds. Decades earlier, I worked with Marcus, a sound-phobic golden retriever who couldn't handle hearing any kind of loud noise, including a truck's backfire on the adjacent highway. Some kids had thrown a firecracker that landed on the formerly confident dog's back. Ever since then, he had gone into an uncontrollable panic at any abrupt sound. The owner called me after Marcus turned the better part of a front door into a pile of toothpicks on July 4. On my first attempt to condition him to accept loud noises, I accidentally taught him to reject pieces of lamb, formerly his favorite food. I had thought the sounds we created (a gun going off over a quarter mile away) would be soft enough, but the trigger overwhelmed the treat, so that Marcus's fear of noise transferred to even the best of snacks. We went back to square one and eventually taught Marcus to be less frightened of loud noises and to go into his crate if the noise still scared him. That experience taught me a lot about starting small and easing a dog into linking the trigger and the treat.

To work on my own reaction to a body scanner, I called up an image from a heavenly vacation when good friends rented a sailboat in the Caribbean. I had been able to lie on my back as the boat gently rolled, hands behind my head, listening to the Beatles singing "Let It Be" while watching cushiony clouds drift across the sky. In the safety of my own home, I practiced bringing that scene and those emotions into my mind as I stood with my feet apart just a little bit, arms raised just a little bit, picturing the sky, feeling the boat, singing along with the lyrics. As time went on, I practiced in the stalls of airport restrooms, then performed muted versions as I waited in security lines.

This would not have helped if I hadn't had years of therapy. But it is why, if you are stuck in line behind me in an airport, you will see me in the machine, eyes closed, trying not to sway to the waves of the ocean and the music of the Beatles, smiling a little as I walk out. And this is why Willie, after innumerable pairings of unfamiliar dogs with food or play, now greets dogs who come to visit the farm with excited anticipation. His body may be a tad bit stiff, just as I am not completely happy to be in a scanner, but neither of us reacts with dread at what used to trigger extreme fear, and both of us get through it to the other side: me to a flight to somewhere, him to an exhilarating run with a new playmate. Willie and I say, "Thank you, Pavlov," from the bottom of our limbic systems.

# CHAPTER TWENTY-FIVE

One January, I was in a yoga center, an expansive room with high ceilings. The winter sun streamed through the windows, gaining strength from the glare of the snow, which lay like a sparkling white bedspread over the grass below. The light ricocheted off the old wooden floor, highlighting the dust bouncing between its beams. The room still held the energy of a thousand souls who had come to buy hardware in this small country town before the building was converted into its present use.

I was talking with my instructor, Scott Anderson, about why so many people didn't do the exercises he advised them to do. This was not a theoretical discussion. For each hour-long session with Scott, I was enraptured by his knowledge of the mind/body connection, soothed by his sonorous voice, and inspired to go home and do my exercises on a daily basis. And then I went home and I didn't. Sometimes I'd do nothing for two or three weeks and begin doing them only a week or so before our next session. Sometimes I'd do them for a week or so and then let myself get caught up in the pull of other things. I'd skip a day, then another, and eventually the only thing I exercised was my ability to feel a vague but pervasive sense of guilt.

The thing was, the exercises that Scott suggested were helping me heal. When I did them, I felt better. I could tell that they strengthened my emotional core as well as my physical one.

The question is obvious: If the exercises made me feel better, why didn't I do them more often? It wasn't because I was too busy. None of us is too busy. Unless you are working in a coal mine fourteen hours a day, you are not too busy to do anything for a couple of minutes a day. Seductive as the "too busy" excuse may be, somehow I managed to find time to read novels at night, to watch television shows too ridiculous to mention, and to have a long lunch with a girlfriend every week. Neither was I lazy. Of all the nasty things a person could call me and be more right than wrong, "lazy" was not one of them. But somehow I found myself struggling on a daily basis to do the very thing that I knew was helping me recover.

It was yoga master Scott and my current therapist, Mare, who helped me uncover the driving force of my intransigence. You know those retractable leashes that tighten as the dog pulls forward? I had my own metaphorical leash attached to my own imaginary collar, pulling me away from the very thing making me feel better. The resistance that was dragging me back from what was good for me was this: If I am no longer the woman whose life is scripted by a series of traumas, then who am I? What would be my story now?

Stories are more than fictional accounts that we read in novels or tell our children to help them go to sleep. Stories are a way of telling ourselves who we are. Our stories can take on lives of their own and write the scripts of many generations. You can be born a Hatfield and revolve your life's narrative around the McCoys. You can be raised in one religion and taught that all others are sinful, while your twin adopted at birth is raised to believe the opposite. Every family has its stories, passed on as powerfully as chromosomes within a DNA spiral. Sometimes these stories are spoken out loud; other times they are passed on indirectly but powerfully, as if by directors who control the action of a play but never appear on the stage. Thus, our own life legends are combinations of the accounts that we inherit from our parents and what we learn from our own experiences.

As important as stories are, we are often not consciously aware of our own narratives. But we should be. As Jill Ker Conway writes in *When Memory Speaks*, "All of us live with a life history in our mind, and very few of us subject it to critical analysis. But we are storytelling creatures. So it's very important to examine your own story and make sure that the plot is the one you really want."

If you don't want the script you're holding in your head and your heart, how do you write a new one? What is more primal than the internal story of your own life, whether conscious or unconscious? Changing your internal identity is as hard as having major surgery on your face without a vision of the result, a random slice here, an addition there, cutting and molding you into something you can't imagine until it's done. Once you look at it that way, resistance becomes understandable, like a friend trying to protect you from grievous harm. After I realized that part of my resistance was the need to hang on to a familiar narrative, I could feel a shift inside, subtle but discernible, like the soft change in light just before the sky begins to glow at dawn.

You can't change your story until you know the current one. Putting words to your life story has tremendous value and can take away the power of a negative narrative. That can be true as much with our dogs as it is with ourselves.

. . . . .

Blazer, a seventy-pound mix of who knows what, crept into my office with his body tense and his ears back. Blazer had the flat, tight coat of a retriever, the muscles of a sumo wrestler, and the dull-brown coat of a street dog. His eyes were black and his teeth glowed in that hyper-white-television-personality way. But his looks belied his behavior. At first he was too frightened to even look at me. It took him a good twenty minutes to come over and sniff my shoes. When he did, I offered my hand for him to investigate, but I was careful not to reach toward him. After a few minutes, he leaned in to my hand and rubbed against it like a cat, then turned and sat quietly while his owner, Margaret, explained that she'd adopted him from a shelter a few months ago.

He'd begun biting her husband three weeks after he was adopted, and now he was charging after men on neighborhood walks. Margaret was quick to defend Blazer. "Blazer was abused by men, I'm sure of it. He doesn't like men, and there's no question he was beaten by one. He pulls away from them every time they reach for him. His previous owner must have been a man who was terribly cruel to him. You know how mean men can be."

"He was abused" are words that trainers and behaviorists hear almost daily, but they often aren't true. Thank heaven for that. If all the dogs who are afraid of men had actually been abused by them, the world would be a more dangerous place than it already is. However, most dogs who become defensively aggressive around guys aren't frightened because some horrible man did horrible things to them. Fearful dogs are almost always more afraid of men than they are women, no matter how men have treated them in the past. We don't know exactly why. It could be the way men are built (big chests and square jaws, the better to bite you with?) or the way they behave (in general, men move more assertively than women), or even the scent of testosterone, but being more afraid of men than women is almost universal in shy dogs. Women especially are quick to have stories as to why. I am reminded of the words written by Gavin de Becker: "At core, men are afraid women will laugh at them, while at core, women are afraid men will kill them."

Blazer and Margaret's story was a familiar one to me. A dog of an uncertain history comes into a new home and is so disoriented and fearful that at first the owners observe no behavior problems. Fear has many manifestations, and one is to suppress behavior, both good and bad. It is common for a shy or undersocialized dog to enter a new home and appear to be a stellar citizen for a few days or weeks. Like people, when a dog is frightened and overwhelmed, he often becomes quiet and compliant, especially if he feels helpless in contexts where he has no control. (Sound familiar?) These quiet, "obedient" dogs aren't inherently well behaved; they are simply shut down. As the dog becomes more comfortable, the constraints on his behavior lessen, and he becomes able to act on his fears. That's when the barking and the growling and sometimes the biting begin.

It appears that was what happened in Margaret's house. Blazer wasn't aggressive to her husband, Ted, at first, but she admitted that the dog avoided him whenever possible. In a "road to hell paved with good intentions" kind of way, Ted attempted to make friends by holding on to Blaze's collar while petting him, not noticing that the dog froze and stopped breathing while he was trapped and unable to get away. Unable to speak, Blazer asked Ted with body language to please stay away, but like many well-meaning dog owners who miss signals of fear in their dog, Ted tried his best to make friends with Blazer by forcing the issue. Sure enough, the first nip was when Ted hugged Blazer, a sign of love and affection to us primates and a rude, threatening action to some dogs. Blazer had finally had enough, and after three weeks, he came out of his behavioral fog to defend himself.

As time went on, the dog gained enough confidence to act on his fears outside the home. He barked and lunged at unfamiliar men while walking in the neighborhood, and he learned that was an effective way to keep scary men away. Inevitably, he got worse.

Margaret came into my office with a story about Blazer, and in her case, it probably wasn't an accurate one. We replaced it with one that was more likely and more effective at changing his behavior. Yes, we needed to acknowledge his fear of men, but it wasn't going to help Blazer if Margaret also perceived them as potential enemies. Margaret was doing a lot of things right, including understanding that his behavior was motivated by fear, and seeking out a coach to assist her in turning things around. However, as we talked, I suspected that Blazer wasn't the only one who had some deep-seated fears about men. While Blazer's behavior wasn't Margaret's fault, her own story about men was getting in the way of helping her dog.

No one can blame Margaret for having a story; we all have stories about our life, including the dogs who share it. How can we not? We are storytelling animals; stories are part of what makes us human. Everyone wants to tell stories about their dogs, me included: I am doing it right now in this book. Because of my profession, I have the luxury of writing about my dogs and talking about them in seminars, lucky me. Others don't have those outlets, and once they learn that someone is a behaviorist or trainer, they cannot resist telling the story of their dogs. They do it on planes, at the supermarket, or when we're at the dentist having oral surgery. I have had people follow me into the restroom and talk to me about their dogs, sometimes even after I close the stall door. I once felt compelled to say, while sitting on the toilet and barraged by a stream of information about someone's five fighting dogs, "I'm sorry, I'm pooping. Could you wait a minute until I'm done?"

But when it comes to our dogs, there are stories and there are stories. On the one hand, there are Mark Twain–like ramblings of the amusing things our dogs have done, whether it is chewing up the dog training book you just bought or humping a pillow when your puritanical aunt came to visit. The other kinds of stories are the important ones—the narratives that define our dogs, giving them a history and an identity all their own. "This is Blazer, and he was abused." "Cleo is the dumbest dog I've ever had." These stories define a dog's identity and frame our expectations. They can help us predict our dogs' behavior and manage the environment to their advantage, but they can also fold our dogs inside of boxes that limit their potential. Just as parents slip into putting their children into categories (Trisha: the pretty one; color = red), well-meaning dog owners often can't resist doing the same.

I would love to tell you that I am above this storytelling, this need to define my dog with a narrative history that filters my expectations, but animal behavior experts are human, too. I've held Willie's story in my heart as carefully as if my hands held a bird that stunned itself flying into a window. This is not all bad. There would be hell to pay if I weren't aware of Willie's history. Years ago he exploded in the vet's office, a barking, frenetic flurry of panic, when he was surprised at the door by a bullmastiff. The dog and owner had left but returned unexpectedly a few moments later and come face-to-face with Willie at the door. All the ingredients of trouble were there for Willie: Tight quarters. On-leash. No way out. Huge dog. Out of the blue.

Willie took one look and burst into wild-eyed barking, but in a microsecond it was over, because I know Willie's story and was always on alert anywhere there might be another dog in a potentially problematic situation. We quickly backed up a few strides; I asked for a watch and then a sit. Willie complied and calmed down. As soon as his face relaxed, I withdrew even farther, teaching him that he could make what scared him go away by relaxing, not by charging forward.

Our stories about our dogs make their lives better in innumerable ways. We buy them padded dog beds when we see that they are aging and their joints might hurt. We arrange playdates with the cocker spaniel next door but avoid the beagle across the street who elicits a growl. Willie may be 98 percent comfortable around other dogs, but I don't take him to dog parks or dog "parties" where he would be overwhelmed by a crush of dogs he doesn't know. I am alert during walks when he may or may not meet an unfamiliar dog, one whose temperament is unknown to us both. And yet I barely pay attention to him greeting other border collies at a sheepdog trial, the context where he is most relaxed and comfortable meeting others of his own species.

· · · · ·

Does Willie have his own stories? No one knows. We know that dogs can't use words to tell us a story, but we don't know if dogs can tell stories to themselves. Can they internally construct a narrative with a beginning, a middle, and an end? Perhaps they can, but not through the use of language. Certainly they can't do what I am doing now as I write and what you are doing as you read. They can't use a series of symbols to help them process events in their past or use them to inform their future. My best guess is that dogs share a need with people to make sense of the world, and perhaps they have some rudimentary ability to construct stories to try to do so. But their lack of linguistic ability is not to be taken lightly, and surely for them this is both a blessing and a curse, just as our own verbal skills both help and hinder us.

· · · · ·

Talking can be a profound help to us when recovering from trauma. In *Trauma and Recovery*, Judith Herman writes that, as long as it done in the right way and at the right time, telling the story of a trauma is an important part of healing from it. Repeating the story over and over gives the events within it less power.

This was true for me. At first it was almost impossible to write about the things that had happened to me. Writing about being molested, being raped, and watching a man die at my feet was exhausting. And horrible. Emotions are contagious, even one's own, and at each revision, it was as though I were reliving the actual event. I wasn't able to quit my day job during this process, and sometimes I found myself reeling during the transition from reexperiencing a rape to running a business or giving a speech about canine behavior.

However, as I retold each event, the power of its effect on me was diluted. It seems that one can use up a story. Like sandpaper, it loses its edge after enough use, and changes from an object that can rub you raw to a mere piece of paper.

And so I will tell you the rest of my story—the part that has been unspeakable for all of my adult life. It is a burden I would like to lay down and turn into just another part of my life's narrative. I am not bored with it yet, but I would like to be.

# CHAPTER TWENTY-SIX

"Trisha, what happened that night?"

The question hit me like a gunshot. My mother and I were sitting at a white-clothed table in a restaurant that overlooked a river in Quechee, Vermont. She had been talking about her English cocker spaniels and plans to redecorate her lakeside home. We'd had some wine and leg of lamb and were sharing a piece of chocolate cake for dessert. My father had died years before, and my mother had moved to New Hampshire to live year-round in a cottage on Squam Lake. I was there for a short visit.

Mom looked down and placed her coffee cup back in its saucer, her bracelets jingling. Her jewelry, always gold, always beautiful, set off her burgundy Burberry jacket. Behind her, beyond the ceiling-high windows of the restaurant, the brown waters of the river churned dramatically over a dam. Except for the sound of the river rushing outside, the restaurant was quiet. Waiters spoke in hushed tones about braised short ribs and halibut on risotto. Glasses clinked softly. The diners beside us laughed quietly. Mom turned her face back to mine, her brown eyes uncharacteristically soft. "I've been afraid to ask you," she said. "But I've always wondered what happened that night."

"That night?" That night had happened over thirty years ago and had never been discussed since. Not within the family, not with my friends; not even in an internal conversation with myself. "That night" had been smothered so deeply by thick layers of shame and denial that at first I didn't even know what she was talking about. I asked, "What night? What do you mean?" But as I spoke, the realization of what she was asking flowed through me in slow motion. My heart stopped beating for a moment and then began to race as my throat tightened. I tried to keep my hand from shaking, but as I put down my fork, it rattled against the plate.

I couldn't answer for the longest time. Suddenly, I was back in the desert, lying in the sand and listening to the owls. Paralyzed. Speechless. I hadn't spoken then about what had happened that night, and I thought I would not be able to speak about it now, with my mother sitting, waiting, staring at my face.

Her question came as a shock. I had been so successful at burying my shame about what I'd done that it had never occurred to me to wonder about my parents' experience of that night, or how they'd lived with the questions they must have had throughout the years.

I looked up at my mother's face and saw none of the black-eyed displeasure that she could express as "Queen Pam," as my sisters and I would sometimes call her. Elegant and noble in so many ways, my English-born and -raised mother could have moments of imperious, pursed-lipped anger. This was not one of them. Her eyes were misty and her face so open and vulnerable that I knew I had to answer her. Initially, I had buried the truth to protect my family, but staying silent wasn't protecting anybody but myself.

"I faked it. I made it all up." My hand, now hidden under the table in my lap, continued to shake. The shaking spread to my body until I was shivering, as if the temperature in the room had plummeted. "I couldn't tell you what had really happened back then. I just couldn't. I didn't know myself why I did it; I couldn't even allow myself to think about it. Now I think I did it because it was the only way I could say that I needed help."

I told her more about that night, how I had looked down at myself as if perched on the ceiling, watching someone who looked like me get ready to drive to the stable. I told her that Bruce had been creeping into my bedroom, just a few feet from her own, and giving me the choice: "Accept having your body violated, or speak up and devastate your sister and your parents."

My mother's face crumpled like a paper napkin. I said, "I'm sorry, I'm so sorry," over and over again. Tears streamed down her cheeks. It was the first time I had ever seen her cry. We both waved the waiter away as he approached, our heads turned away from him and each other, looking out the window at the roiling river. I said nothing to her about the man who fell nor about being raped a decade later. It was too much for her to hear. It was too much for me to tell.

Pale and shaken, we sat in the restaurant for the longest time, tears flowing down our faces. It broke my heart to see my mother so upset. What mother wouldn't be devastated to learn that her daughter had been molested in her own home, just a few feet away from her? We must have said "I'm sorry" to each other a hundred times. Finally, the waiter, who had studiously avoided us for the last half hour, gathered the courage to bring us the bill. We left the restaurant, heads held high, putting on a good face, willpower propelling us to the car in the parking lot.

My mother did not hug me; she was never a hugger. She didn't like being touched, not even by her own children. I knew that she loved me deeply, and I also knew that my family's mantra—that a stiff upper lip can get you through anything—was no longer going to work.

· · · · ·

Within days, I found a counselor, Anne Simon Wolf, who may not have saved my life, but she helped me save myself. I was lost for a while in a fog of recovery, and I'm not sure where I would have ended up without her. I told her my story, the whole long, nasty truth of it. I poured out my guilt and shame in between gulping sobs that engulfed my body. Anne didn't ask questions; she just listened. After my words began to slow and my crying began to wind down, she began to respond.

She explained that what I had experienced the night I faked the kidnapping was called "disassociation." It is a relatively common effect of severe trauma in which one detaches from one's self, as I had that night in the kitchen. Being molested, and watching a man fall through the air and die at my feet—while being part of a family in which troubles were to be soldiered through silently—had caught up to me. By faking the kidnapping, I was reaching out in the only way that I knew how. Giving voice to what was happening at the time was impossible to contemplate. You have to believe that you have a choice in order to make one.

I also told Anne about the rape in Minneapolis, although I had never thought of it with anything but shame. How could I call it a rape? It was my fault, pure and simple. Yes, I was still reeling from my marriage falling apart; yes, I was desperate to feel lovable and attractive and to be able to laugh and enjoy being a woman with a man again. And no, I did not give him permission to overpower me and flip me upside down like a rag doll and hurt me more than I believed to be physically possible. But really, rape? No stranger had leaped out of the bushes with a knife and threatened to kill me if I didn't submit. The loaded gun in the bedroom may have sat next to my head, but he never picked it up.

But the guilt and shame over the sexual abuse was nothing compared to my guilt over faking a kidnapping. In my mind, I had switched from victim to perpetrator, and initially, I found the knowledge unbearable.

. . . . .

Once my story spilled out to Anne, I felt as though I'd slammed into my past at a million miles an hour, as if into an impenetrable wall. Have you ever seen powerboat races, the kind in which boats go up to 250 miles per hour until some tiny thing goes wrong and the boat explodes as if hit by a bomb? That was me: Trisha the exploding boat. The term "fell apart" had an entirely new meaning for me now. It felt like "I"—whoever that was—was strewn about in the water like the result of a dramatic crash. Sometimes you don't find all the pieces.

I was dumbstruck from the shock. I couldn't sleep. I couldn't think. I canceled my appointments for the rest of the week. I felt like some metaphorical bottom had dropped out from underneath me and I was falling into an infinite abyss. I had no sense of where I was, who I was, or where I fit into the universe anymore.

The day after I told my therapist the entire story, I sat on my couch in a state of emotional intensity that was unbearable. I called Anne and told her I kept thinking about leaping in front of a car; that I was positive that I would not and yet was equally sure that I could not bear to live another minute feeling as I was.

She got me through that hour, and then I lived through to the next, and then the next.

I blurted out to the people in my office that I'd been raped—that was the easiest story to describe. Karen London, a PhD animal behaviorist doing consults in my office, showed up at my door with flowers. I hope I thanked her—her kindness meant the world to me—but I might not have. I found myself unable to speak after having finally given voice to much of what had happened in my past. After a few days, I was able to function, and I read voraciously about sexual trauma. Mostly, I cried so much it was hard to see the print on the page.

This happened when I was living alone at the farm. In some ways it was good to be alone; to let my sobs turn into screams without needing to censor myself for the sake of others. It was also hard to be alone, but really, I wasn't. Willie's uncle, Cool Hand Luke, lay beside me night after night, licking my face, curled up against me. His warmth and his love helped me to pull out of the high-speed emotional spirals, staying alive one breath at a time.

• • • • •

I would like to tell you that after the truth about my past came out, I was soon able to process it and move on. On the contrary, all of my fears became conscious ones. I became more afraid of being alone, of entering the dark barn at night, of loud noises that came out of nowhere. I lost the ability to sleep well, managing a few hours a night at best. I had nightmares and flashbacks and was jumpy and exhausted. As Anne told me in one of our talks, "There is a reason why people repress things."

But I kept at it. I wrote in a journal every morning. I saw Anne often, and although the sessions were exhausting, they were helpful. Anne suggested that I name and describe the voice inside me that saw the world as a place of relentless danger. I named her ONO, because she reacted to much of life by saying "Oh no!" just as my father had. Anne suggested that I name all the personas within me and sit back while they had a conversation. It might sound a bit crazy, but in reality, it was the opposite. We all have different parts of ourselves that are often in contention, and as with the boy who cried wolf, ONO's cries of warning were so frequent that I had tried to ignore them for decades. "What if ONO was right? That there really are dangers lurking around you?" said Anne. "What if ONO could stop yelling all the time if she was taken seriously?"

I named and described all the different aspects of my personality, from the academic who loves logic and algebra (Margaret, short, clipped hair, always wears biological brown) to the brave warrior woman (Xena, long dark hair, wears leather and has biceps like a rock climber). These two and several others sat down and let ONO speak. "You have to listen to me!" ONO said. "Haven't you all figured out how dangerous life can be?" Margaret, Xena, and everyone else did indeed listen and thanked ONO for providing an important service. "You are right, the world can be a dangerous place, and it is good that you are there to keep us alert." They also reminded her that she was not alone. That Xena the warrior woman was always there to protect her. That Margaret could logically analyze situations and decide when real trouble was on the horizon and when it was a false alarm.

This exercise helped me immensely. I became less fearful once I learned that the frightened voice within me would stop yelling once I listened to it. When a sense of panic began to rise up in me like water on a rising tide, I learned to gather the facets of my personality and listen to what they had to say. "Yes, ONO, we hear you. Entering a dark barn at night can indeed be scary; that's a perfectly reasonable fear. It probably reminds you of the rape. But has anything ever happened in all the years you've walked into your barn alone at night? And wouldn't your dogs notice first if there were someone inside? Why don't you open the door and send one in first if you're feeling nervous?"

These imaginary conversations were not so magical that they transformed my life. I doubt there is any one thing that can help those who are recovering from multiple traumas. But accepting everything that was inside of me, especially the fear I had squelched for decades, made life profoundly easier. It was only one part of what I did during my recovery—which included the Hoffman Process, practicing yoga, meditating, and telling my story—yet it helped. A lot.

· · · · ·

However, life continued to remind me that you never close the book on dealing with your past. You just keep reading the chapters over and over, until you begin to understand them on a deeper level.

# Chapter Twenty-seven

In early 2010, Lassie died of liver cancer. Just days afterward, I found myself sitting at the computer, searching on the Internet for another dog. After any of mine had passed away in the past, I hadn't been able to think about another dog for a long time. It took two years for me to get another Great Pyrenees after my first one died. And while it simply is not possible to love a dog more than I loved Lassie, it was different this time. I'm not sure why. True, I couldn't rely on the often injured Willie as my working sheepdog, and I also wanted him to have another playmate. But there was a yearning inside me to get another dog that I still can't quite explain. Being without Lassie was like a sentence without a period, a sip of liquid without a swallow.

Finding a good match for Willie wouldn't be easy. Just like relationships between family members, some interactions between dogs are sweet and easy, others prickly and difficult. Hundreds of my clients have had a well-behaved, happy dog until a newcomer came onto the scene and blew the household's contentment out the window. Granted, at four years old, Willie was profoundly improved. Few would believe that his behavioral problems had been so serious, because now he got along well with a variety of dogs. His best friends included a huge Doberman, the Serena Williams of dogdom, who told him once in no uncertain terms to stop trying to herd her. Willie flattened his ears and grinned like a schoolboy and thereafter worshipped the ground she walked on. He loved visits from the sweet, submissive border collie Max; they'd race each other up and down the swales of the orchard pasture, running shoulder to shoulder like Thoroughbreds on a track, tongues lolling, eyes bright as water droplets. Willie went on country walks with a pack of dogs with minimal management. At times he and another dog would posture and things would begin to look tense, but a quiet "Let's go" would break the ice.

Indoors, it was a different matter. It's common for dogs to be more comfortable where there is room to maneuver, and Willie could be fine with a dog when they were outside. But once he was in the house, his eyes would harden, and he'd flick his tongue in and out like a snake testing the air. "Tongue flicks" are often signs of low-level anxiety in dogs; you can see them in the lobby of any veterinary clinic. And in this case, size mattered. Large dogs made Willie so nervous that I stopped asking them into the house while we worked our way up the scale. The smaller the better, as far as Willie was concerned.

So, after Lassie's death, it seemed wise to get an adult lap-sized dog; or, if I wanted another border collie, to start with a puppy.

I searched all the shelters and rescue sites, but nothing showed up that motivated me to check further. The dogs either chased cats or fought with other dogs or, for some reason, didn't grab my heart. I kept at it sporadically, and eventually, a good friend mentioned a breeding of two working border collies who were famous for their good dispositions. The puppies from previous litters were reported to be bombproof—lovely with people, good with other dogs, and good working dogs besides. My plan had been to rescue a little lapdog first, then complete the picture in a year or two with another border collie. But here was a potentially great litter of sheepdogs, calling to me to check it out.

Finding the right pet dog can be a challenge, but it is particularly difficult to find a dog who is both a great companion and a competitive working sheepdog. I have had innumerable clients who wanted help in their search for a "one-in-a-million dog" to replace the one they had. After they listed their criteria—friendly with people and all other dogs, no behavioral problems, healthy, always obedient, nonshedding, tolerant of grandchildren—I had to remind them that one-in-a-million dogs are just that. By definition, we know the odds of finding another one.

I knew enough not to ask for perfection, but after twenty-three years working full-time with dogs who had severe behavioral problems, six years of dealing with medically challenged elderly dogs, and years of working with Willie, I needed a dog who wasn't going to present extreme challenges. Not a perfect dog; just a normal one who needed patience and training but didn't need extensive physical or behavioral therapy.

First and foremost, the dog had to get along with Willie. After hearing raves about the parents and siblings of the upcoming litter, Jim and I drove a few hours north to meet the parents. I'd known the father dog for years and loved him for his stable benevolence. Mom-to-be was tiny and squiggly-sweet; as soft as silk around people; and a force to be reckoned with around sheep. Everything suggested that this litter could produce a great pup for our family, so back we went two months later to pick one out. We left Willie at home to avoid the overwhelming cacophony of barking dogs, and because I wasn't confident he'd behave appropriately around a litter of puppies.

We settled on a tricolored pup named Mick. He cheerfully left his littermates to follow us away from their pen, and paid little attention to the wind slapping the leaves around in the trees shading the grass. He leaped after a thrown piece of paper like a coyote on a field mouse, picked it up, and returned it to me, eyes glowing, tail wagging.

I liked the looks of him, I liked the genetics of the litter, and I liked the way he responded to everything we did. I picked him up and asked for just one more test. Given Willie's extreme reaction to unfamiliar dogs, it seemed wise to see how the pup behaved around dogs he didn't know. I asked the breeder to let out a dog whom the pups had never met. The litter stayed inside a large circular wire pen set out in the open while an unfamiliar adult dog was allowed to run up to the pen and greet them. All the pups ran to the fence to say hello, tails thumping back and forth, whining with excitement. Except one. Mick ran to the center of the pen and sat as still as a statue. *Damn. Okay, take a breath; maybe he'll relax.* But no, as the older dog ran circles around the pen and the rest of the litter followed him like particles of iron being pulled around by a magnet, Mick stayed motionless, head down, mouth closed tight.

As the wind continued to blow, Jim and I sat in the car and talked about whether we should take Mick home. Everything looked so good except for this one red flag. How important was it? After going back and forth for thirty minutes, we agreed to take the pup home for a three-day trial to see how he and Willie got along.

When we got home, we let the pup explore the yard a bit before letting Willie out to meet him. Willie's reaction was all you could hope for—he met Mick with a relaxed body and a loosely wagging tail. Mick's reaction, however, was déjà vu all over again. He was terrified of Willie. He slammed himself to the ground, yipped in terror, and tried to run under the car. I stood still for a moment, trying to breathe normally, my heart sinking. Was I going to go through this all over again? Spend three or four years working on getting a dog to behave normally, as I'd done with Willie? *Too soon to say,* I reminded myself.

We let Mick become accustomed to Willie as the afternoon shadows lengthened and the sheep came down with their lambs for the evening grain. By nightfall, Mick was approaching Willie for attention. Good! By the next morning he was mounting him. Relentlessly. Mounting in general doesn't worry me; puppies and adult dogs do it often in play, and unless a female is in heat, it is related to social relationships, not reproduction. It is a behavior you'd expect to see between puppies or two older dogs, but a tiny pup mounting an adult male just hours after meeting? *Hmm.*

More problematically, Mick didn't look like a dog mounting another during play. He did it with an intensity that was chilling. He looked like an adult dog breeding a female in estrus. Experienced stud dogs don't mess around—they take an evaluative sniff every time they pass the female, and if she's ovulating, they hop on and clasp the female's hindquarters with locked forelegs. As they penetrate the female, they pin their ears to their skulls, squint their eyes shut, and flick their tongues in and out. There's nothing playful or even pleasurable-looking about it. The dogs look focused and serious, as if they have a difficult job that requires all their attention and concentration. That's exactly how this tiny dog looked: serious. And grown up. It looked very, very wrong.

He did it continually, obsessively, and Willie did nothing

to stop him. If Willie had just snarled him off, it might have stopped there, but Willie stood looking downtrodden and help-less while it happened. The dog who insisted on full control over interactions with adults became as helpless as a newborn lamb around a puppy. I intervened when I could, but every time I turned around, it began again. In all my years of working with dogs, I couldn't remember seeing a pup this age behave in the same way.

What should I make of it? Was it predictive of trouble down the road? There's no way to know for sure if it was an indication of problematic behavior later in life. However, a young pup who is both terrified of unfamiliar dogs and behaves like an adult male at eight weeks of age around familiar ones is not within the bell curve of normal.

At times like these, we behaviorists wish we knew less. Ig-norance truly can be bliss, and I wondered at every moment whether we should keep Mick or not. On the one hand, Mick was almost a dream dog when away from Willie. In under two days, he'd mastered sitting and lying down on cue and was learning to walk politely on a leash. There was one exception: He urinated more often than any puppy I've ever had. Although I took him out every ten minutes, he'd pee in the house in a heartbeat, barely pausing to squat while the urine flew out from underneath him. It was frustrating and time-consuming but hardly a deal-breaker. Border collies are famously easily to house-train, so after getting the all-clear from the vet, I expected the issue to resolve itself soon.

However, Mick's behavior toward Willie was relentless and atypical. I asked friends and colleagues in the dog world, "What would you think of a young pup who was acting like Mick?" Most of the responses were "Take him back yesterday"—not because he was a bad dog but because he seemed a bad match for Willie.

No matter how dedicated and skilled you are at training, you can't fit round pegs into square holes, and sometimes behavior problems are as much about a bad fit as a lack of skill or knowledge. That is as true with dogs as it is with people. Ask yourself if you could marry anyone randomly picked off the street and be happy. Or sane. This is not an excuse to pass dogs around like casseroles; most behavioral problems can be solved with training and behavior modification. But the fact is, a small percentage of dogs are in environments where they simply are never going to be happy. Dogs cannot speak their misery, and it is up to us to translate their expressions and actions into words. If they are telling us that they are miserable where they are, it is our responsibility to find them a place where they can flourish.

As hard as it was, I accepted that Mick was not a good match for Willie, and I drove him back to the breeders on a cold and windy day. Mick ended up in a great home the same day I returned him. I wasn't sure whether I'd return home with another puppy from the litter. Their genetics were so solid that it was tempting. This time I brought Willie with me to check out the rest of the litter, because his appropriate greeting to Mick suggested that I could trust him around the pups without weeks of gradual introductions. I brought out a big-boned male puppy who was a perfect replica of his stable and benevolent father. Willie made snake eyes at him, stiffened, and immediately withdrew. Darn, he had been my second choice. The only one left was a male who had tested relatively well in the puppy tests but whom I had rudely labeled "ugly puppy." It seemed wrong not to give him a chance, so I hoisted him out of his pen and took him outside to meet Willie.

It was love at first sight. Willie immediately play-bowed, the pup groveled and squiggled, and in seconds they were romping and playing in an ice-cold driving rain. After watching them in apparent bliss for twenty minutes, I picked up the pup and drove him and Willie home.

For three days, we were all in heaven. I named the pup Hope, a common name for both male and female sheepdogs but equally symbolic of my need to find the right dog for Willie. He and Hope played joyfully. Hope's head and ears began to develop, so he became cuter. He was responsive to Jim and me, a quick learner, and tremendously fun to train.

I then wrote a lengthy blog about why I had returned the first pup. I wrote honestly about the process, in hopes of helping others in similar situations, and because the issue of "the right dog" is an important one. No matter how much someone loves dogs, that person's home is not always the best place for any one particular dog. You can't mix oil and water or gasoline and matches. The most responsible thing to do is to acknowledge when a dog is mismatched and find a way for him to end up in the best possible place. After I published the blog, the vast majority of readers wrote to thank me for writing about why I'd returned Mick, and for my courage in writing about it honestly.

The word "courage" was mentioned often; one would have thought I had single-handedly battled off an attack of terrorists. But they knew the kind of criticism that I'd soon be facing, and they were right. Some of the comments were nasty. I was called a hypocrite and a failure as a behaviorist. Someone suggested that no one in her group would read any of my books ever again.

A faction of people in the dog world believes that rehoming a dog is tantamount to tossing it out the window on a highway and that the only responsible course of action is to keep a dog you've brought into your home, no matter the circumstances. Ironically, many of these same people foster dogs through rescue groups, keeping the dog if it fits in to their family, but sending the dog to another home if it does not.

Even though I knew I'd be criticized for returning Mick, even though I had taken him on a three-day trial basis, I was emotionally exhausted after three days of "Should I or should I not take the puppy back?" I had already fallen in love with Mick when he wasn't around Willie, and taking him back felt like a love affair gone wrong. The criticisms felt both personal—we were talking about my family, after all—and professional. Although I responded to the criticisms as constructively as I could, and my skin had been thickened over the years by being in the public eye, I still felt as if I'd been publicly whipped.

The support of Jim and my best girlfriends and the joy of having Hope in the house saved me. Willie and Hope played together beautifully, mock-wrestling on the living room floor, playing tug games with Uncle Willie, who modulated his power to match that of the pup. Hope was crazy fun to train—as smart and responsive as Mick—and for three days, we were all having a ball.

Until we weren't.

Day four of life with puppy Hope began with a sweetheart of a morning, rich with the melodious song of rufous-sided towhees. "Drink your TEA TEA TEA!" they sang as I did the chores with Willie and Hope at my heels. The dogs played inside and out, and soon Dr. John, our "James Herriot by another name" veterinarian, came out to give the pup a vaccination.

Hope licked John's face rapturously, and Willie pushed in for equal attention while Dr. John cooed and kissed and gave Hope a shot so quickly he barely noticed. We went outside to chat and take the pup to pee. After relieving himself, Hope pounced on a stick and ran under a bush with it. John and I were talking a few feet away, and I happened to turn my head in the pup's direction as Willie walked over to investigate. Like a bullet, Hope shot out toward Willie, eyes blazing, lips snarling, with a growl more appropriate to a full-grown dog than a baby pup. Willie stopped, as stunned as I was, and turned away.

And thus began the Summer from Hell. Hope began bullying Willie, leaping up and biting the top of his neck any time Willie moved from one place to another. As he did so, he let out a series of growls that led me to call him "Psycho Pup." The snarls were lower in pitch than a pup his size should be physically able to produce, more appropriate to a horror movie than a living room. If Willie had simply corrected him with an appropriate snap, it probably would have ended there, but for some reason (as with Mick), Willie seemed incapable of defending himself. Willie, who, as a pup, hadn't hesitated to challenge an adult dog over a vegetable, was unwilling or unable to discipline the tiniest of puppies. It made little sense that a dog who could be so aggressive in one context could be so helpless in another.

But then I'd remind myself how we are all different in different contexts. Perhaps Willie was following the unwritten "puppy pass" policy that seems so common in canines, in which rude behavior is tolerated in young dogs, just as it is in very young children? Or perhaps I had conditioned him so carefully that I'd taken away his ability to assert himself? Either way, in spite of all my efforts, I felt as helpless as he was behaving, and it added yet another layer of angst to a summer filled with worry.

Like his littermate, Hope urinated more often than other

pups and seemed oblivious to standard house training. The vet discovered that he had crystals in his urine and cleared those up, but his relentless need to potty continued over the summer. Normally, this would have been no more than irksome, but I had fallen a week after bringing Hope home and smashed my knee, so I was on crutches and in a lot of pain. Far worse, Jim had popped his bicep tendon off the bone while helping a stranger load heavy objects into her van, and he had to wear a burdensome arm brace for months after surgery to repair it. He had only one good arm, and I had only one good leg—not an ideal situation when living on a working farm with a puppy who needs to go outside a gazillion times a day.

Besides these difficult logistics, a soul-sucking angst ate at me every day. On the one hand, Hope was a dream puppy to train. Teaching him something new was like paddling a canoe down a river—you had to exert some effort, but you always knew the current was going in the right direction. You could even pick up the paddles sometimes and just let yourself coast. So much of the training I had done for the last two decades was on older dogs with serious behavior problems; I had almost forgotten how glorious it is to work with a pup. Any time we were out of the house, we had a wonderful time—in puppy class and on walks in small towns where strangers would squat down to scratch his chin and he would squint in bliss.

But inside, the tension between Hope and Willie was so dense it felt hard to breathe. They had stopped playing together, and every time Willie got up to go from one room to another, Hope leaped onto his shoulder, growling and snarling like an adult wolf during breeding season. Willie would nervously flick his tongue and continue moving forward as if Hope didn't exist. Silent interventions from Jim or me only delayed the next attack, and verbal corrections would have intimidated Willie as much as the pup. Outside, the tables were turned. Every time the pup began to run forward as if to play, Willie would muzzle-punch him into a stop. Willie apparently thought that this was great fun, the puppy not so much. Instead of playing joyfully, they had to be watched and managed constantly while I attempted to foster a good relationship between them. On crutches, with a bum knee, and a disabled husband.

*It'll be fine*, I told myself. *I'm an animal behaviorist. I can work through this. Hope is just a puppy.* I consulted colleagues. I wrote out a treatment plan, complete with goals, expectations, and step-by-step instructions. The best plan was to teach Hope a different response to Willie's movement, so that every time Willie got up, Hope would come to me, or go get a toy, or log on to the Internet and order expensive dog toys. Anything to keep him from bullying Willie, who behaved like he was incapable of growling at a tiny puppy. The training helped, but not enough. Hope was obsessed, seemingly driven to harass Willie, or at least to respond to his every movement by attacking him.

Jim and I agreed that the best course of action was to work on their relationship over the summer and reassess in a few months. All the time, every day and every minute, a silent but relentless internal voice told me that, like Mick, Hope was the wrong dog for Willie. Hope was a lovely pup who would be better off with a group of normal dogs who would benevolently teach him manners. Willie deserved to have a safe home where he wasn't being bullied. Both my knee and Jim's arm needed to heal. I waited and worked on Hope because it seemed right to give him some time.

But that wasn't the only reason I put off making a decision. I knew I'd get criticized on the Internet for returning another puppy. This time I wasn't sure I had the emotional strength to put up with it. Not just because I would be criticized but because I was criticizing myself. I wasn't sure I'd made the best decision when I brought Hope home. The decision to bring home Mick had been made thoughtfully and carefully. However, in Hope's case, I'd taken one look at him and Willie playing in the rain, picked up the pup, and put him in the car without further thought. I could have driven home and thought about it. I could have put the pup away and gone inside the breeder's house to ponder. Even though I had carefully researched the genetics of the litter, deciding to take home the pup I had rejected earlier felt like a snap decision. The breeder and the friend who'd come with me had looked at me in shock when I declared that I was taking Hope home, knowing that I'd shown little interest in him beforehand. Still, it seemed like a good decision for the first three days. But after a few weeks, it became clear that yet again, this was not the right dog to add to our family.

· · · · ·

Perfection is unattainable—no dog is perfect, and of course, no person is either. Yet, like many, I often fight the belief that I should be free of mistakes, and I suffer from shame when I come up short. But this emotion comes in many shades, and ever since I pretended to be kidnapped, a black veil of shame has been my silent but constant partner for over fifty years.

We all feel shame about some things in our lives, and most of us bury it as deeply as we can because it is so painful to experience. Getting rid of guilt is difficult (admitting "I did a bad thing"), but getting rid of shame ("I am a bad person") is even harder. The power that it has over us derives from our tendency to keep it hidden. Shame is a private, intimate thing—no wonder rape and shame go hand in hand—and yet it loses its grip on us only if we bathe it in light.

Brené Brown, author of *Daring Greatly*, has studied the emotion of shame for years. She found that, in general, men universally feel ashamed if they are perceived as weak, whereas women tend to feel shame about not "being perfect." Somehow men have come to believe that they must be all-powerful, all the time. Women believe that they need to be perfect professionals, perfect mothers, perfect lovers with perfect bodies . . . and to never have a problem puppy. Or get molested or raped. Or pretend to be kidnapped. Until I went into therapy, I tried never to think about any of it. It was as though, every once in a while, a mass of deep water would recede enough to let the memories surface, but then it instantly would rush back in and cover it up.

Exposing our private shames to the light does not require us to reveal all of our deepest secrets to everyone. We may be living in a culture in which people exchange privacy for fame, but that doesn't mean it serves them to do so. Brené Brown has found that people living what she calls a "wholehearted life" are resilient to the destructive power of shame because they handle it as if dealing with a toxic chemical. Exposing one's shame without any thought of a safety system is as dangerous as handling nuclear material without a containment plan. There are rules about when to disclose and when not to: Don't go public about something you are ashamed of until you have worked it through privately. Be sure that you have a safety net of friends who will be there for you no matter what. Learn to dismiss criticism from those who aren't "in the arena" or haven't been in a similar situation.

I didn't know any of that when I wrote about bringing Mick

and Hope to the farm. I had the safety net of true friends, but I wasn't wise enough (in my relentless imperfection) to heed points number one and three. The bad news is that it was painful. The good news is that I learned a lot.

· · · · ·

The public reaction to my story about Mick and Hope was a vaccine against the reaction I feared if I exposed my darkest secret about faking a kidnapping. Intellectually, what I did makes all the sense in the world: A young girl could not bring herself to say out loud that a series of events had left her ashamed, as well as being terrified that another version of doom could occur at any moment. And yet it is one thing to tell the world that you've been raped or molested, given the shame our culture still attaches to its survivors. It is another thing to come clean after lying about something as horrific as being kidnapped—which makes you the perpetrator instead of the victim. And it is another thing entirely to learn how to forgive yourself for it.

# CHAPTER TWENTY-EIGHT

Saint Bernards are big dogs, and the one in my office was a very big dog indeed. Merlin must have weighed 160 pounds, with a head as big as a volleyball. There are advantages to owning a dog the size of a pony. You can stroke its head without bending down. People wave and smile as they see you walking by. However, the dog's size also means that he can drag you across the street until the skin of your forearms is scraped off by the asphalt, as Merlin had done to his owner, Joyce. Joyce couldn't have weighed more than a hundred pounds, so it was easy for Merlin to pull her around like a toy on a string.

Being dragged across the pavement by a large dog is the stuff of cartoons and sitcoms. We laugh because we can relate—what dog owner hasn't once been the victim of an out-of-control pet that turned us into a slapstick wagon careening down the street? In a slip-on-a-banana-peel kind of way, it's amusing to see others lose their dignity to something we can't always control. Joyce told me that people often laughed at her as her massive dog dragged her somewhere she didn't want to go.

Except it wasn't funny. Merlin wasn't enthusiastically chasing a squirrel up a tree or dashing over to the neighbors to play with their children. Merlin was using every bit of his power to attack any dog in his line of sight. Several times he had managed to overpower Joyce and injure other dogs, even though Joyce had equipped him with a special collar and harness to control him.

As Joyce told me their history, Merlin sat nobly beside her, strong and fit, his eyes radiating quiet dignity. If he could talk, I'm sure he would have said, "Don't believe a word of it."

Joyce had done all she knew to stop his attacks. She had tried to train him to sit and stay when he saw another dog, and she walked him at odd hours to avoid other dogs. All of this had helped a little, but the week before our appointment, he had bolted after another dog and sent Joyce flying onto the gravel, badly injuring her arm and shoulder. Without the help of a jogger, she never would have been able to stop him before he reached the other dog.

In spite of her own injuries, Joyce was primarily afraid that Merlin would hurt or kill another dog. But fear wasn't the only emotion she was experiencing. She also felt guilty. And ashamed. And embarrassed. Guilty that her dog had a serious behavior problem she couldn't manage. Ashamed because she felt she'd failed as a responsible dog owner. Embarrassed because being hauled like a hay wagon in front of the neighbors was humiliating.

Joyce was not alone. The dark side of being a responsible dog owner is being plagued with guilt and its handmaiden, shame.

Guilt isn't necessarily a bad thing. Feeling guilty isn't fun, which is why it prevents us from repeating something we've done in the past that is best not done again. But guilt and shame can be two-edged swords. I've had a multitude of clients who felt so guilty about their dog's behavior that they were almost paralyzed. I learned to say, "I know that your dog's behavior is problematic, but I do want you to remember that you yourself didn't bite anyone." Even clients whose dogs merely growled at a suspicious stranger told me how bad they felt about it. Or that their family dog of thirteen years wasn't getting along with the new dog they'd rescued from the shelter.

However, nothing compares to the guilt that dog lovers feel when forced to make the decision to have their dog euthanized. Despite moving heaven and earth to save their pets, many owners are wracked with guilt over putting their dog down to relieve its suffering. It breaks my heart, because I, too, know the burden of guilt associated with taking away the life of one's best friend. I was overwhelmed with guilt when Luke died at age twelve from kidney failure, sure that if I had just tried hard enough, I could have saved him. The fact that five of the best veterinarians in the country couldn't save him was irrelevant to me. I was his human. He was my dog. He had risked his life to save me from horned creatures who could have killed me; how could I not save him in return?

· · · · ·

Guilt is an equal-opportunity employer, affecting us in all aspects of our lives. Nowhere is that more evident than in the aftermath of sexual assault. Survivors find a multitude of reasons to feel guilty, from blaming themselves that it happened in the first place; to feeling guilty that it wasn't "bad enough" to be upset about; to believing that if they were better people, they'd be fine by now.

For years, when I allowed myself to think about it, I asked myself, *How could I have possibly gotten myself raped and molested?* (That is the way I asked the question—"gotten myself.") Surely, both events must have been my fault. In some ways I was lucky that I kept quiet about what happened for so long, because it spared me from being blamed by others, a common occurrence after a traumatic event. Some version of blaming is almost universal, no doubt because it assuages the fears of nonvictims: "That wouldn't happen to me, because I would make a better choice." You can almost hear them say "whew" in relief.

While "You're guilty (and I am not)" can provide solace to others, "I'm guilty" has its own benefits. If you yourself are guilty, then by implication you had some kind of control over the situation—and heaven knows, we all want to believe that we are in control. Perhaps the most frequent words I hear as an animal behaviorist are, "If only . . ." "If only I had remembered to shut the door, my dog wouldn't have run outside and been hit by a car." "If only I hadn't taken him to the park that day, he'd never had gotten in that horrible fight."

*If only*. Seductive words, because they protect us from facing the far more frightening reality—that stuff happens all the time over which we have no control. Bad stuff. To good people. And good dogs. It just does. That is why it's comforting to believe that if we had just done X or not done Y, the horrible event Z would not have happened.

Sometimes, of course, there is some truth to the "if only" game. If only I had been strong enough to walk out of Jason's apartment the moment I saw the gun in the bedroom, I probably wouldn't have been raped. If only I had been able to tell my parents or my sister that Bruce was coming into my room at night, the intrusions would have stopped sooner. But that is not always the way the world works. We don't always make the right decision. Stuff happens no matter what we do—there was nothing I could have done to stop a man from falling out of the sky and dying at my feet. And covering myself with a heavy blanket of guilt couldn't change any of it.

· · · · ·

It took a long time for me to get over the death of Willie's uncle Luke. He was otherwise brimming with health, exuding a vitality that no dog I've had has ever matched. I fought the reality of his untimely death daily for years after he passed away. *If only* I had figured out why his kidneys were failing. *If only* I had been a better person, a better dog owner, a better animal behaviorist who knew how to get my dog the best possible medical care.

Luke's headstone is at the top of the farm road that leads to the pasture high above the farmhouse. It is a rough-hewn slab of granite that sits in the grass where Luke used to wait for me to catch up with him so that we could work sheep together. He would stand on the hill's rise, silhouetted by the sky, and turn his head to me as I walked up the slope behind him. "Are you coming? Hurry! I see them! They are there, over there. Can I go get them?"

In the years after he died, sometimes I'd sit down beside his grave with no purpose except to be close to what was left of him. One crisp fall day years after his death, when I was still fighting the "if only" battles, I looked at the words engraved on his headstone: "That'll do, Luke, that'll do." These words, in sheepdog speak, tell the dog that his work is done for the day. I put them on the headstone to tell Luke that it was time to let go of his responsibilities. Your work is done now, Luke. That'll do.

As I sat in the sun and listened to the crickets buzz, I suddenly felt as if Luke were standing behind me. Of course I knew he wasn't there, but I still felt him standing in the grass, looking at me with his usual bemused expression. The feeling was so strong that I couldn't resist turning my head to look behind me. There was nothing there but grass and sky. My eyes rested on Luke's headstone as I turned back around, and I read the words on it as if for the first time: "That'll do."

*Oh. Okay.* I stood up and felt layers of guilt shedding off me, as if I had just entered a warm house on a cold day and removed a heavy coat. I let go of my guilt over Luke's death, as well as much of my guilt over what had happened in my past, and left it lying on my good dog's grave. It was the last and best gift that Luke ever gave me.

· · · · ·

In late summer, I found young Hope another home. He had begun barking fearfully at unfamiliar people and dogs, not an uncommon problem for an adolescent border collie. I had no doubt that I could help him through it—it is a phase that often disappears if handled correctly—but his behavior began to affect Willie. Willie's problems had been too serious, and the idea of losing the ground I'd spent years gaining was untenable. As much as I didn't want to give up on Hope (oh, the irony of that phrase), it became clear that he wasn't helping Willie or me. Loving Hope wasn't reason enough to keep him. Neither was being afraid of what people would say.

The decision was made the day when both Hope and Willie barked aggressively at a sweet elderly woman walking down the street. Willie had a host of problems, but a fear of an elderly women walking toward him wasn't one of them. Hope's fearful behavior was contagious, and I could not allow Willie to develop another problem behavior.

As often happens, the universe provided. I found Hope a

wonderful new home within days. I felt grief over his departure but also a deep sense of relief.

A few weeks later, we ran into him at a sheepdog trial. Hope was happy to see me but ran back to his new human with glee, obviously enthralled with his new family. Willie's response was to take one sniff of Hope, turn his back, and sit facing away from him. After that, he refused to look in Hope's direction. I suspect that guilt was the last thing on his mind.

# Chapter Twenty-nine

One fall day, Willie was standing stock-still about two hundred yards away from me in the field, behind three sheep who would rather have been somewhere else. He had run his gorgeous wide outrun to the back of them at a sheepdog trial, but now he stood motionless, looking directly at me as if he had no idea what to do. I whistled to him to Walk Up, to put his head down and take charge of the sheep, which he did every day on the farm. He'd done it at other sheep trials, like all the other border collies competing, knowing full well that their first job is to get around behind the flock and bring it to you, no matter how far away. But this time Willie wasn't doing the work. He wasn't doing anything. While I whistled for him to get moving, he stood immobile, looking at me as if he had just woken from a deep sleep and had no idea where he was and what he was supposed to do next.

Dogs don't always listen at sheepdog competitions. This is hardly a surprise to anyone who has ever owned a dog and called for Chester or Misty to come into the house instead of rolling in a puddle in the backyard. What is surprising is that sheepdogs listen so well. The dogs work far away, off-leash, and using nothing more than a series of words and whistles, we ask them to stop, speed up, go right, or circle left around a group of fast-moving animals. The dogs can be three hundred yards away, or five hundred yards, or even half a mile, in some of the rarefied trials far beyond the ability of mere mortals like Willie and me. A quiet whistle is all it takes to bring the sheep back into a straight line or slow the dog from a trot to a walk to keep things under control. The dogs love to work; they crave it like a drug. What's more, they want to work as a team with you.

Of course, dogs and handlers aren't perfect, and sometimes when a dog ignores his handler, the handler switches from whistles ("Tweet, tweet!") to words ("Walk Up!") to something outside the usual repertoire ("HEY! Are you listening to me?").

Handlers who are watching often smile when they hear these phrases of frustration. We've been there. We know that an unresponsive dog is either listening just fine but choosing to ignore his handler ("I've got this, just shut up and leave me alone") or is too panicked to take in any information ("Oh God, I'm out here all on my own, and the sheep are going to get away any second now, and I can't let that happen, and I can barely think, much less listen"). But I've never seen a dog at a trial stand behind the sheep with his head up as if he had virtually no idea what to do next.

Willie's indecision went on for an eternity. I whistled, I called, and I whistled again. He stood as if transfixed, looking straight at me from two hundred yards away. Eventually, the sheep drifted off on their own, and Willie began to follow them. Finally, he woke up and took charge of the flock, responding to my every signal, and brought them straight to my feet. We were about to begin the driving portion of the course when the lead ewe, an old girl who had seen more than her share of sheepdog

trials, flattened her ears and bolted off the course. Willie tried to contain her, but she knew she had him beat. Willie knew it, too. I suspect she'd figured him out at the beginning, when he abdicated responsibility; she'd just been waiting for an opening. I called Willie, and we walked off the course.

I felt awful. Sick-to-my-stomach awful. I wasn't angry at Willie, although I was sad and confused, I felt an outpouring of love and sympathy for him that was overwhelming. He'd looked so helpless.

I was also embarrassed. All handlers have had a dog not listen to them at a competition, but I knew no one whose dog stood motionless while the handler whistled, yelled, and flapped her arms to no avail. I felt helpless, too. Why had he just stood there? What had I done wrong?

When things go poorly, it doesn't help to have a reputation as an animal behaviorist. Two people, bless them, had come up to me during the trial and said, "Oh, you're Patricia McConnell! I've read all your books, and I love them! You're my hero!" Right before Willie and I ran, a nationally famous trainer came up and said hello, loaded down with a new massive camera lens, all the better to record our run. Ouch.

Afterward, I ruminated for a couple of days. I had some ideas about why Willie had done what he did. He probably hadn't been able to hear me and was afraid to act on his own. He had become more hesitant and less confident after his year of immobility when his shoulder was hurt. His personality made him easier to handle during his recovery than many dogs would have been, but it also meant that his sense of autonomy was easily squelched.

After his shoulder was healed, I put him in a few small sheepdog trials where he did well at the beginner's level, although he

seemed to have a new kind of hesitancy that I hadn't seen before. The next summer he strained his iliopsoas muscle and had to go back on-leash for three months. That might have been the last straw in Willie's sense of independence. After he recovered, he began looking back at me more often while working sheep: "What should I do now?" I encouraged him, buzzed him up, let him drive the sheep faster than usual to make it fun and exciting, to keep him focused on the sheep and not me. He got a bit better, although there were still times when he would stop and turn to look at me: "Okay? Am I doing okay?"

That may have explained, at least in part, why Willie did what he did: a stiff wind had come up that made it especially difficult for him to hear me, and he was hesitant to take initiative without hearing my signals. However, the sick feeling in my stomach didn't go away after I had sorted out the probable causes of his behavior. My distress felt out of proportion to what had happened. Willie hadn't done well at a trial. He probably couldn't hear me because of the wind. So what?

Perhaps I was feeling distressed because I was humiliated by our performance. It is never fun to fail publicly, but it may feel worse when others have high expectations. Sheepdog handlers know that the skills that I used to work with aggressive or panicked dogs have little to do with training and handling a working sheepdog in a competition, but the public doesn't know that. People often expect my dogs to be nothing less than perfect in every situation.

I remember one morning when my dogs flushed a deer while we were on a walk in the woods with friends. The doe bolted away within a few feet of us, her white tail erect and waving from side to side like a flag. The dogs shot after her, at full speed within two or three strides. I sang out, "Lie down!" and they hit

the dirt as if they had fallen out of the air, and what was more, they did it happily. I teach a "flying lie down" as part of play, so the dogs had learned that it was fun to lie down as fast as they could while running away from me. Still, I was filled with pride and gratitude that morning. *Look at how good they are! I'm so proud of them!* I thought. The people walking with me didn't even pause in their conversation. "Of course your dogs would be that good," they later told me when I asked them about it. "What else would we expect from the dogs of a professional dog trainer?"

Still, disappointment and humiliation didn't seem like the real reasons that my gut was in a knot even days later. As I lay miserable at two in the morning, I did the only thing I could think of. As the moon shone through the window, I began the loving-kindness meditation: "May I be safe. May I be healthy and happy. May I live my life in peace."

I'm a lazy meditator, and I tend to meditate only a few minutes at a time, in awe of people who spend fourteen hours a day at retreats in painful positions while focusing on nothing but their breath. After repeating the few sentences for a mere five minutes, I suddenly saw the word "helpless" in my mind and realized that I had found the core of the problem. Whenever I told my friends what had happened, I had described Willie as "looking so helpless" and myself as "so helpless, standing there at the post."

*Helpless.* I must have said that word a hundred times. Willie looked helpless. I felt helpless. Helpless, like when a man fell out of the sky and died at my feet. Helpless, like when I was raped by the Vietnam vet. Helpless when someone I had trusted as a young teenager violated me in my bedroom and took away any sense of security that I had. That was the problem: Feeling helpless is awful. This was not about Willie; this was about me.

• • • • •

Here is what I am learning about trauma: It is not something that you can close the cover on and then put it away like a book on a shelf. Recovery is an ongoing process that requires courage, honesty, and a kick-ass support system. Whatever happens to you during and after a trauma doesn't disappear as if it never happened. It just gets easier to deal with, if you know how to face it. Stuff comes up—it will *always* come up—and you have to look it in the eye and back it down, like a dog standing nose to nose with a ram. But you can do that if you've done the work beforehand, if you have a good support system, and most important, if you have faith that what you need is inside you. You just have to take the risk to find it.

• • • • •

Willie ran in another sheepdog trial not long after the one where he'd frozen in place. I almost didn't attend, worried that he didn't want to compete anymore. But he'd done well at a clinic between the trials, so I decided to try one more time before retiring him from competition.

Each dog entered in the trial got two runs. In Willie's first run, he began with a wide and lovely outrun, gently got the sheep moving, and brought them in a dead-straight line to me. Almost perfect. We worked together to drive them away in another straight line to freestanding gate panels about a hundred yards away. Everything was going beautifully. And then Willie stopped again and didn't move. At least I assume he stopped. He was out of sight, behind a copse of trees, but I could see the sheep standing still for the longest time. They finally wandered into a thicket of willows surrounding a stream. I had to leave the post, walk a couple of hundred yards across the field, and work with Willie to herd the sheep out of the thicket. He had to push them across a deep creek, the water up to his shoulders as he pushed them back toward the field. I was perplexed by why he had stopped again—I suspected because he couldn't hear me again—but this time I saw it as an interesting intellectual exercise rather than as reflection of my worth as a person or a metaphor for feeling helpless.

Willie kicked butt on his second run. It was our best run ever. We worked together seamlessly as partners: He was precise and responsive, and I timed my signals (finally) so that the sheep moved in perfect lines around the course. It was gloriously fun. There is little as seductive as the feeling that your dog, the sheep, and you are all in the same groove—your dog using his power and maturity to move the sheep gently and carefully through a prescribed course; the sheep relaxing as the dog takes charge; you using your experience and timing to help your dog be at his best. When it works, it feels frictionless, like the kind of mental "flow" that psychologist Csikszentmihalyi talks about—a state in which you are completely, blissfully absorbed in what you are doing.

· · · · ·

Lesson learned: I will never finish dealing with trauma. But when I take the risks necessary to face it, I get better and better at it.

# CHAPTER THIRTY

The farm. It calls to me when I'm away, like some organic siren song that won't stop, a tree-lined tinnitus always singing in my ear. Twelve acres of wild geraniums and dandelions, wild deer and domestic sheep, the farm becomes a single entity to me when I am gone. It won't let me go.

The farm is my most important therapist. I told Jim when we first began dating to never ask me to choose between him and the farm. Every day I give thanks for being able to live in the country, and every day I savor the peace that only nature can provide. My farm is nestled in the Driftless Area of southern Wisconsin, a region skipped by the glaciers that bulldozed much of the state into flat plains. The land is a rolling pastoral mix of woods and pastures, fields and streams. It is simply lovely. Frank Lloyd Wright once said, "Nothing picks you up in its arms and so gently, almost lovingly, cradles you as do these southwestern Wisconsin hills."

It's not always so benevolent. One summer, there'd been a drought and a heat wave for months on end. It had been like living in an oven. The wilting roadside plants broadcast the weather report on a daily basis, and the crisp brown grass began

237

to crackle under my feet as I walked to the barn. The neighbor's soybeans curled up and began to die. Each individual cornstalk in the fields surrounding the farm looked increasingly desperate. Corn is a grass—just a big, tall one—and when it is starved for water, the normally fat green leaves turn silver and skinny, stretching upward with spiky tips like pineapple plants. It was painful to watch them degrade as the hot, dry days went on, the sun beating down as in a movie scene titled "Guy dying of thirst crawls through the desert sands under the scorching sun." By the time the rains finally came, the pasture where the sheep used to graze was mostly dirt. It was hard to imagine that not long ago it had been a lush, tiny forest of Kentucky bluegrass and white clover, wetting my shoes with dew as Willie and I walked the sheep to the orchard pasture in the morning.

The dogs and I were confined inside much of the time, the heat so extreme that going outside was a kind of physical assault. The sheep lay in the barnyard like dogs in the tropics, flat on their sides, legs extended, desperate to disperse whatever heat they could. People began selling off their livestock. I didn't take my usual walks, or work Willie on sheep, or weed the perennial garden. I used what little energy I had to save the trees, hauling hoses from one end of the yard to the other.

Yet as brutal as living with the land can be, I wouldn't trade my connection to it for anything. Sometimes I think I owe my life to it. It might seem strange to talk about the healing force of nature, and how it has helped me specifically, by telling a sad story about the effects of a drought. But it is not just beautiful flowers and awe-inspiring vistas that do a body good.

Living in the country includes sprained ankles, wasp stings, sunburns, and droughts that break your heart. It means bitter winter nights in the barn, trying to save a dying ewe gasping for air, her eyes rolling, her chest heaving, while your fingers are so cold they sting like fire, or extracting a deer whose leg caught in your fence only to learn she was killed the next day by a neighbor's dog.

But I love it still. I love the good and I love hating the bad. The fact that the farm is not all pretty and comforting somehow makes it even more valuable. One day there's the shocking finality of a dead newborn lamb in the barn. The next day the healthy ones frolic, my spirits rising with them as they toss their heels to the sky. Bearing witness to the inevitable link between the living and the dead helps me to feel centered, with the earth holding me up and the land surrounding me with something bigger and better than my own little life.

· · · · ·

I'm not the only one who values the natural world. Our universal attraction to life on earth is visible everywhere you look for it. Hotel rooms with a view of trees or water cost more than those that don't. Homes with bushes and mature trees are worth more than those without them. We cherish flowers and send them for comfort after the death of a loved one, or to celebrate a victory, or to woo a mate. That's an amazing range of contexts, if you think about it—comfort, congratulations, and courtship.

This attraction to plants and animals is therapeutic in many ways. We know that spending time outside decreases the incidence of depression and anxiety in children, increases their scores on standardized tests, and, according to one report, makes them "nicer" to others and enhances social interactions. Viewing a nature video speeds recovery from stressful events in adults. Living next to a park or even having a tree outside the window reduces domestic violence. Spending time out-of-doors reduces stress and mental fatigue, restores mental clarity, and increases one's sense of well-being. Richard Louv, author of *Last Child in the Woods*, sums up the value of being in nature: "These are the moments when the world is made whole."

What the research rarely mentions is that spending time outside isn't always pleasant. Anyone who camps on a regular basis knows what it is like to huddle inside a tent for hours on end while the rain dumps down in buckets. The beauty of a pristine forest can be hard to appreciate when there are clouds of mosquitoes hovering around your face. That is especially true of farming, where the weather, the plants, and the animals decide your agenda, and you have no choice but to comply with their demands. A difficult lambing cancels your plans to see the play you've had tickets to for months. Spring planting can't be put off until summer because you hurt your back. No matter how impressed we humans might be with our superior intellects and skills, we don't get to call all the shots. That's not always a negative. It's not such a bad thing to have a primal understanding that we are not above nature but a part of it.

· · · · ·

You don't have to live on a farm to retain a connection to nature; perhaps nothing gives us the same sense of connection with the rest of life on earth as dogs. Although our relationship with them is no less than a biological miracle, it is a mixed bag. Dogs bring us joy one moment and a mouthful of cat poop the next. They make us laugh, and soothe our souls, and destroy the quilt our grandmother made especially for us. Sometimes they lick away our tears in the morning and bite our faces in the evening. The balance between happiness and hardship varies, depending on the dog and the home into which it has come. Some dogs bound into our lives as pure light, a living version of television's Lassie, enriching our days and warming our nights. Others come with baggage and, like many of the dogs I saw as a behaviorist, cause us no end of problems. But no matter who they are or how they behave, dogs have become our most important connection to the rest of the natural world. They become a part of our families, and yet they have teeth that can rip open a deer hide. They sleep on our couches but lure us outside, alerting us to the squirrel in the tree, the dead earthworm in the grass. One moment, they swell our hearts with love, just as a sunset fills us with awe. Minutes later, we grimace in disgust as they smear their shoulders with the stink of dead fish. But like our connections to the rest of nature, being with dogs makes us whole. It doesn't have to be pretty all the time to do that.

· · · · ·

My relationship with Willie wasn't always pretty. At its darkest time, it barely seemed worth it. But somehow I knew that Willie was not only my connection to nature, he was my connection to my deepest self. Knowing one's self is not always sweet sunrises and daisies waving in the breeze, either. Sometimes it is thunderstorms and drenching rain, or a morning so bitter cold that the air burns your lungs. But when you have a dog, you have to go outside no matter what the weather. Willie taught me that as long as I was dressed for the weather, I'd be glad I went.

· · · · ·

Every summer, barn swallows chitter just a few feet away from my study, skimming the air currents, landing precariously on a rope we strung up on the porch for the attachment of holiday

241

lights. When Willie and I go outside, the birds swoosh away and begin swooping over the grass to snatch up more insects. Last spring a swallow nested in the garage, her nest built of mud and fiber on top of a light fixture. It was a foolish choice, because each day I'd leave the farm and close the garage door, keeping the parents either shut out or trapped inside while I was gone. I'd drive back up to the house, press the automatic door opener, and the adults would swoop in or out, squawking in what sounded like avian anger, desperate to get to the nest or out to feed. After a few days, I left the garage door open, unwilling to witness the slow death of a poorly placed clutch of baby birds.

Each day the chirps of the babies got louder, and soon they were so big their bodies leaked over the edges of the nest, like a blousy woman overflowing her bra. They began flapping their wings and leaning precariously into the air. I worried they would fall before their wings were strong enough to hold them. I kept the cat inside, and while she paced and yowled behind the door, I talked to the birds: "Hurry up, it's time to move on."

And then one day when Willie and I left the house on our morning walk, all five baby birds were straining so far out of the nest that I knew their first flight was inevitable. One at a time, they dived out and flapped in sloppy circles all around us, their movements uncoordinated and seemingly inadequate to keep them aloft. At the last minute, as they descended closer and closer to the ground, their wings took hold, and they managed to stay airborne. They fluttered for a few more seconds, seemingly at the edge of disaster, and then slalomed out of the garage and crash-landed into a nearby spruce tree. But they took off again, and gradually, flap by flap, the movements of their wings became more coordinated. Their paths through the air became cleaner, more purposeful.

They began to dip and turn, faster and faster, until within just a few minutes I was surrounded by five expert flyers, zooming right and buzzing left, streaking toward my face and banking away at the last minute, so close I could see their eyes shine. Willie and I stood together, still and silent, smack in the middle of the most amazing air show on earth, performed by five miniature pilots with the right stuff. As they swooped and soared around us, they appeared to be overwhelmed with the beauty and power they had inside themselves all along—they just had to take the risk to find it.

# Chapter Thirty-one

Forgiveness is something you can't force. It has to be approached indirectly, like two dogs avoiding eye contact while they greet each other in carefully paced semicircles. It began for me by first having the courage to acknowledge all that had happened and seeking help to resolve the aftermath. I then had to acknowledge a red haze of anger and fear, each like a mythical monster imbued with the power to eat me alive.

However, dragons can be slayed; that's why we made them up. But first you have to face them.

In part, I found forgiveness in hearing the stories of others. Listening to my friends tell their stories filled me with compassion and made it easier for me to feel compassion for myself. There can be no forgiveness without compassion, which is no doubt why it is a key tenet in the world's religions.

However, it is harder to forgive ourselves than it is to forgive others. We are hardwired to remember negative events over positive ones, so we ruminate on our mistakes and the slights of others. Our ability to use language means that we can spend hours mentally criticizing what we did in the past or worrying about what we'll do in the future. No wonder we love dogs, who don't need meditation retreats to get over the shame of getting into the garbage last Thursday.

What dogs can't do is tap into the knowledge that they are not alone; that they can be special as unique individuals and yet be a part of a whole that cradles and supports them. The solace I got from hearing the stories of others came in part from learning that my reactions to trauma were common and understandable, and from the sympathy and compassion that flowed between us. Bathing myself in compassion for others helped me redirect some of it toward myself. Talking to vibrant, intelligent, and accomplished women who had survived sexual and physical violence inspired me, awed me, and began to chip away at one of the darkest effects of being a victim of trauma: hanging on to one's "victimhood" as a way of feeling special.

We are a culture that idolizes "special." Our children need unique names now, or if they have a common name, they need to spell it differently. I did a book signing once in Los Angeles, and a man asked me to sign the book to him. His name was Bob. Except he spelled it B-o-b-b. The same need to be special exists among some dog lovers. Dogs adopted from neighbors or as retired breeding dogs are "rescues"; simple behavioral problems are explained in hushed voices with the words "I know he's been abused." But being special isn't all that it's cracked up to be, because what comes along with feeling special is feeling different—which makes it all the harder to feel the strength that comes from sharing one's experience with the rest of the world.

Dogs can't have discussions such as this, but perhaps they don't need to. Their lack of language keeps them better connected to the universal truth that we are all a part of a bigger whole, and that the boundaries between "me" and "others" are not as clear as we humans often think. Language may be much of what makes us human, but putting our experiences into words creates a kind of distance from them, a form of simultaneous translation that is never quite the same as the original.

Language, however, was an important part of what helped me find my way to forgiveness. My therapy sessions with Anne and Mare changed my life. My sister Wendy, whose boyfriend molested me, has cried multiple times with me about what happened and has stood by me like a warrior woman on the road to my recovery. So has my other sister, Liza.

After I told my mother what had happened "that night" and why I had done it, she began to open up to me about her own life in ways she never had before. She had endured her own traumas, including barely surviving a historic fire at her boarding school, Battle Abbey, in which she and her classmates made it out of the conflagration with seconds to spare. The roof caved in behind them as they marched out of the building, the flames from the fire so high they were seen for miles. My mother was the only girl whose parents did not come to take her home the next day, believing the headmistress's admonition that she'd be "fine, just fine" without any help from her family. It all sounded so very familiar.

She repeated this story often as she lay dying in 2004. Clearly, it had been one of the most defining events of her life, and yet she never got the chance to acknowledge her terror and her sense of being abandoned. All she had was the belief that she should bury the memory and be strong, using nothing but the force of willpower to get her through each day.

I was lucky. I had so many resources that she never had. Sometimes I conjure her up as a little girl, wild-eyed and alone with the sky in flames behind her. I hold her in my lap and tell her she's not alone, just as sometimes I imagine myself at fifteen and tell the confused, frightened girl that it's okay. It's okay.

. . . . .

Somehow, after facing what had happened to me and learning how to rise above it, I began to sleep again. I had barely slept at all for eight months after my mother asked me what had happened, and years later, Willie's excessive startle response had set me back to sleeping only a few hours at a time. But gradually, all the work began to pay off, and I began to sleep through the night again.

At some point, I stopped feeling—no, knowing—that someone was about to slam a baseball bat into my head. Not long ago I was walking down a street and realized with surprise that it had been a long time since I'd been compelled to turn around so the faceless man with the bat would disappear. Nor do I envision my home and dogs burned to ashes, as I did for years every day when I drove down the road that flows like water toward the farm.

. . . . .

My life now has changed in other ways. I don't see clients anymore. I write and I speak about animal behavior, but I am done working with aggressive dogs. I loved it, thrived on it, but twenty-three years of it was enough. Although not every one of my cases came to a successful conclusion, I helped thousands of dogs and the people who loved them, and I am grateful to have had that opportunity. In part, I stopped because I am slower to react now; I don't have the reflexes I used to. But perhaps as important, I no longer feel the need to face my fears in the same way I did before. Psychologists know that people seek out familiar situations, even when those circumstances are dangerous or abusive. And there I was, putting myself in danger every day, working with dogs who could have badly injured me if I made the wrong move.

But in that case, unlike in my past, I wasn't helpless. In my work with aggressive dogs, I had knowledge and skill and, in a short period of time, enough experience to face the threats and turn them around. Perhaps that was why I loved working with fearful dogs even when they were dangerous. Not only did I empathize with them, but I was able to deal with danger in a context where I had control.

That didn't mean I was fearless. Early in my career, I called John Wright, one of the country's first PhD animal behaviorists, and blurted out that a black-eyed standard poodle had scared me to the core when he began leaping up to my face and snapping at it. "That's good!" John said. "Listen to your body; it will tell you if you are in danger. Don't ever be afraid of being afraid."

Working with dogs taught me, as well as anything else, about listening to that inner voice and facing my fears rather than running away from them. I learned to reclassify my own fear as valuable information that I could use to change a dog's behavior. I began to sense early on when a dog might be dangerous to me and when it was not, to figure out what the dog wanted or needed, and to use that to change his behavior. When that little voice inside of me—the little voice that I spent so long trying to ignore—said, "Be afraid," I learned to welcome it and thank it for the information. I learned to carry the fear while relaxing my body and breathing deeply when I was nervous, signaling the dog to relax, too. I learned that you could be frightened and get away with it—as long as you didn't run from the fear, and you learned how to control it.

In turn, I saw so much fear in many of my clients' dogs. Rather than interpreting their behavior as "dominant" or "aggressive," I could see they were terrified, and that their behavior—whether it was biting or hiding in the corner—was the only way they knew to control what was happening around them. As I learned how to acknowledge and deal with my fears, I learned how to help them deal with theirs.

At one level, being a behaviorist is all about control. Control of your body, control of your emotions, control of the dog's behavior, control of the client's. I realize that sounds a bit draconian—especially given that the word "control" is often used now as a pejorative description. What woman isn't afraid of being called a "controlling bitch"? But the fact is that we all want and need control. Much of growing up is learning to control our impulses; most of our social behavior is about controlling—uh, influencing the behavior of others. Describing an attempt to get your child to come home before curfew or your partner to hang up his clothes as "controlling" may make us uncomfortable, but that is indeed what we are all trying to do: control our environment in a way that makes our life better. Or safer.

Trauma survivors understand this in a way few others do—that a sense of control is essential to one's humanity, and the loss of it is like losing yourself. Helping someone regain a sense of control is critical to turning him or her from a victim into a survivor. The opposite of being in control is being helpless, and that's the last place that trauma survivors need to go back to. My work taught me to acknowledge fear, to use it and control it, instead of letting it control me.

Like us, dogs need a sense that they are not helpless victims; that they can have an effect on the behavior of others around them. Dogs can also be traumatized, in ways that profoundly affect their behavior. I now believe that many of the dogs I saw as clients were victims of some kind of trauma, whether from an attack by another dog, from abusive treatment by a previous owner, or from being pulled from the horror of a puppy mill. It is time to view them as we see survivors of war or of sexual and physical violence—not as examples of deficient individuals who should be blamed for their inadequacies or need for "dominance" but as individuals who can be healed through skill and compassion. These dogs need, first and foremost, the patience and understanding that provide them a sense of safety, and the belief they can have some influence on the world around them.

• • • • •

I see Willie as one of those damaged individuals, even though I have no idea why he came to me as if he'd experienced some horrific event within the first weeks of his life.

I have often wondered if I projected myself onto Willie, and my own fears elicited much of his behavior. My answer varies from day to day. *Sometimes. Probably. A little. Maybe a lot.* He showed himself to be remarkably fearful and reactive when he first arrived on the farm, but that doesn't mean my own issues didn't exacerbate his. If I have projected my own fears onto him in ways that I have not done on any other dog, then perhaps the universe arranged for him to come to me when I was ready to face my deepest fears. Sometimes I believe things like that happen. Sometimes I don't.

All I know for sure is that young Willie arrived at the farm as if his brain were on the verge of panic at every moment. Through careful repetition and conditioning, he learned that he could control his environment in a way that kept him safe. He could get the "scary thing" to go away if he either stayed calm or looked at me instead of barking hysterically. Once he discovered that he had some control over the behavior of other dogs, he began to associate their approach with something good. Like everyone whose nervous system is stuck on alert, Willie needed both his internal and his external environment to change to rewire his brain back to normal.

No wonder we love each other so much.

# CHAPTER THIRTY-TWO

It is late summer now, and the crickets are so loud this time of year that a visiting city friend once said, "My God, what a racket!" The only other sounds are from the three dogs who live at Redstart Farm: Willie, Tootsie, and Maggie. Willie is panting after a long run up the hill with young border collie Maggie, who is sprawled on the floor, her tongue lolling from running in the heat and humidity of a midwestern summer. Tootsie, a tiny Cavalier King Charles spaniel, is snoring loudly on the couch.

Tootsie arrived in 2012, after my unsuccessful attempts to find a second border collie to be a playmate to Willie and a backup sheepdog. I settled on finding a small lapdog who needed a home, and Tootsie fit the bill: As a docile female, she had a good chance of being accepted by Willie, especially since some of his good friends had been Cavaliers. After seven years of pumping out babies in the nightmare scenario of a puppy mill, Tootsie was rescued by the good people at Lucky Star Rescue and needed a home. Tootsie is resilience personified. Even after seven years in a crate little larger than a bread box, she adores people and is as calm as Willie is reactive. Tootsie's motivations in life are clear: 1) Eat all the food you can; and 2) Live as much of your life as possible sleeping on something soft, preferably a person.

I couldn't help her with unlimited food, since that would be no better for her than for the rest of us. But she snuggles in bed with me and Jim, and warms my chest and calms my soul when I lie on the couch every evening. She never startles when a truck goes by or if the breeze rattles a limb against the window. I call her my oxytocin pump. Tootsie gets lap time every evening, but as the night progresses, Willie and I still have our own private cuddle session. After attempting every night to insert herself between us, Tootsie gives up, walks up the tiny stairs that Jim built for her so that she can get up onto the couch herself, and takes yet another nap.

Of course, no one (and nothing) is perfect. Willie and Tootsie have lived together for years now, and after one brief and uneventful meeting, they do not acknowledge each other's presence. In spite of my hopes that they would play together, they do not look at each other, sniff each other, or behave as though they have noticed that there is another dog in the house. On rare occasions one will surreptitiously sniff the other, then instantly turn away lest they get caught doing it.

Twice during her first year here, I caught Willie glaring at Tootsie with a tense face and hard eyes, a look that I am sure even a mill dog can interpret as trouble. But he didn't repeat that behavior and accepted her into the house, even if he doesn't interact with her. Willie ignores Tootsie's barking, her incessant pushing in for attention, and even lets her climb onto his shoulders to get closer to our faces during greetings. He appears to perceive her as something one would rather live without but that takes little energy to tolerate, like stopping at a red light in traffic when you're not in a hurry. I am grateful that they get along, if one can define "getting along" as pretending the other doesn't exist.

After six months of training, Tootsie was housebroken. (One of my finest hours as a behaviorist: It is no small accomplishment to teach a small dog to never go in the house after pottying in her own bed for seven years.) She is also trustable off-leash in the yard if carefully watched (finest hour number two). She is not, however, the dog she would have been if she had been raised in a good home.

One of the symptoms of psychological trauma is "emotional numbing." There is a part of Tootsie that is shut down, as if a closed window has swollen shut after a rainstorm and can never be opened. When I look into her eyes, something seems to be missing, although I can't say exactly what it is. On the other hand, after months of standing in the backyard, confused and disoriented by the complexity of sights and sounds outside of a puppy mill, she discovered that she is a spaniel, and that the world is rich with the scent of squirrels and field mice. Watching her blossom into an actual dog from a sweet but traumatized puppy machine has been one of my greatest joys in life.

But now, two years after Tootsie's arrival, there is another dog at Redstart Farm: Maggie, a four-year-old border collie, a small tricolored cutie with one ear up and one ear down. Maggie came to us after I spent two years looking for our next border collie, and months of discussions with her first owner, a well-respected sheepdog trainer in Idaho.

Jim and I were gobsmacked in love with Maggie at first glance. She was everything we'd hoped she would be—sweet, smart, and responsive. But things did not go well when she first met Willie. It was not because of Willie. By then all the work that he and I had done together had paid off, and I simply never worried about him when he was greeting new dogs unless he was trapped in a small space.

But I had to force myself to breathe normally when the dogs first set eyes on each other. Was Maggie going to be the right one? Was the third time, please, please, going to be the charm? We let the dogs greet in a big fenced field, with lots of freedom and no sense of pressure. Willie trotted over on his toes, all Mr. Excited Anticipation, like a guy at a bar with high hopes and a fake gold chain around his neck. Maggie bolted away from him. Jim and I ignored them and kept walking down the grassy slope. Willie, bless him, used everything he'd learned over the years and responded perfectly. He turned away and peed the equivalent of a Facebook page on the frozen grass.

Maggie was too frightened to take the bait and sniff where he had urinated, but we kept walking forward. In a few minutes Willie tried to approach her again, stopping when she darted away. This time she didn't run as far. We continued this dance for a hundred yards down the field, where Maggie finally stopped, turned, and looked directly at Willie. He turned to face her and dipped his body in the slightest of play bows. They stood for a second, staring at each other. Jim and I stood still, too, mesmerized, and then Maggie play-bowed to Willie and took off like the Road Runner fleeing Wile E. Coyote, her back legs running faster than her front ones. Willie ran after her, then she after him. For a good five minutes, they ran huge looping circles around the pasture, mouths open, tongues lolling, as happy as two kids sledding down a hill together, while tears streamed down my face because finally, finally, Willie had found a friend he could play with, and we had our third dog, and I knew, just knew, that she was the one.

If this were a movie, that's where it would end, with the music swelling and everyone's heart in their throat. But life never works that way. As expected, Willie became tense when encountering Maggie in the house, his eyes going flat when he saw her, even if she was in another room. Maggie was afraid of him if he came too close, even when he was being as polite as possible outside in the yard. She was even afraid of Tootsie and the cats for a few days. Although she had been well socialized to other dogs, she had never been away from her mother and her packmates, and I've learned that this makes a huge difference in a dog's behavior. But nothing about her behavior was out of the bell curve; she was simply lost and afraid in a new environment without her family and friends around her. Everything I'd learned over the past decades told me that once she found her confidence, she was the right dog for Willie. The little voice inside me said, "It will be okay."

It was. It took three short weeks for Willie and Maggie to become best friends. At first we used crates, gates at the doors, and leashes to keep them from being too close to each other in the house. We let them loose together only in the big pasture at the top of the hill, where they would run until their sides heaved and their tongues curled like spoons. We took them on leash walks into the village, where they forgot about being too close to each other while sniffing the urine marks of other dogs.

Now they are family. They play tug games several times a day, and walk side by side on the trail through the woods, mutually exploring the scents of passing deer, rabbit, and raccoon. They run together in boundless circles, Maggie dancing in front: "Ha ha! That was fun! Chase me again!"

In the evening, Maggie comes over to Willie and paws at him or tries to lick his face. Sometimes he gets up and plays tug with her. Other times he wrinkles his lips and tells her to go away. She does. Maggie's temperament, along with her experience growing up in a pack of dogs, has resulted in brilliant social skills. Willie, on the other hand, had to overcome his own temperament, a hindrance to him in his early years rather than a help. However, all our work together resulted in a dog who knows how to respond with finesse rather than panic if another dog irritates him. That doesn't mean he isn't capable of being rude. He tries to herd Maggie while they're playing, and he will nip at her face to try to stop her if we don't make sure he has a toy in his mouth. He can get grumpy when he is tired.

He is also an idiot. There really is simply no better word for much of his behavior. As I write, he is recovering from serious injury number six. Or is it seven? I'm losing track. Even at the age of ten, Willie still uses his body like a drunken high school boy at his first rock concert, exuberant and out of control, slamming down the aisle of life as though he is immortal.

When I bottle-feed the lambs, Willie lies in the barn outside the pen. He would like to dash back and forth behind the gate, but I tell him to stay there while I do the chores. He does, but his body is tensed like a drum. As I leave the pen and come through the gate, I say, "That'll do, Willie." He could then stand up at a reasonable speed, turn around, and trot with me out of the barn. Or he could do what he does—simultaneously rise while throwing himself in a 180-degree turn and take two ground-gulping strides, all in under half a second. It is both impressive and ridiculous. If there were an Olympic event for Getting Up While Turning Around and Taking Two Strides in the Least Amount of Time Possible for No Reason Whatsoever, Willie would have the gold medal. There's a price to pay: It's tough on one's body to live every moment of life as if in the finals of a life-changing athletic event. His body has paid the price for having an internal engine always set on "smoking."

Until recently, watching Willie teeter on the brink of physical disaster exhausted me. Every time he leaped or slid or smashed into something, I'd gasp, my limbic system on red alert that something horrible was about to happen. But that was then, and this is now. Now I shake my head and say, "Oh, Willie," and hope that he hasn't hurt himself yet again.

There is another important change in his behavior aside from becoming comfortable with other dogs: Willie no longer startles out of a dead sleep for no discernible reason. This behavior had become rare after years of our work together, but it stopped completely within weeks of Maggie's arrival. Perhaps, along with all the work we did together, he needed just the right dog in the house to feel truly secure. Our dogs may love us, but surely we are still aliens to them, creatures who constantly confuse them with our strange greeting behaviors and relentless need to go on long, slow walks while ignoring all interesting things. Something about Maggie's presence has soothed Willie in a way that nothing else ever could. I wonder if Maggie is to Willie what Jim is to me—both of them inherently stable individuals who allow us more nervous types to let our guards down.

There's no question that Willie loves Jim as much as I do. In one way, Jim is the opposite of Willie and me. Willie and I are the wind and the fire and the wildflowers; Jim is the earth and the water and the stately oak tree that stabilizes us both. I can't imagine how I could love a dog more than I love Willie, and I believe that Willie loves me like life itself, but we cannot be for each other what each of us needs at our core—a sense of stability and security that allows us turn off our vigilance, take a deep breath, and nestle together, safe and secure.

Jim and I got married in 2012, after twelve years together. The little voice inside me finally said "Yes, yes" instead of "No, not again."

I said yes to Willie, too, when I pledged to face my own deepest fears so that he and I could heal together. For that, I owe him more than I can say. If not for his fears and reactivity, I might never have been forced to deal with my own deeply buried past. I love him so much that my heart aches just saying it, even though sometimes I still have to go out of my way to forgive Willie for being Willie. But I have, and I do. When he crashes into the car that has been parked in the same place for the last four years, or strains yet another muscle while scrambling up from lying down, for no reason whatsoever, I say "Oh, Willie. My Silly-Billie Willie-boy."

· · · · ·

Now, late in the evening, after the chores are done and the dishes are washed, you will find the five of us settled in the small living room in our old farmhouse. Willie and Maggie are lying side by side on the rug after a long, noisy tug game. Jim and I are on the couch, Tootsie snoring on my chest, my feet snuggled under Jim's warm legs. Maggie lifts her head and licks Willie's face. Willie is tired and wrinkles his lips the tiniest bit. Both dogs put their heads back down, roll onto their sides, and go to sleep. Tootsie, lying with her too-cute face and tiny white paws on my chest, is snoring like a three-hundred-pound drunk passed out on a bar. Jim turns his head to look at her, and we smile at each other as the crickets continue singing the sonata of life and the moonlight streams through the farmhouse window.

# Epilogue

It is hard to send your dog to gather sheep you cannot see. It is one thing to send him down into a valley where you watch as he flows through the grass in a wide, open circle to the other side of the flock. It's another thing entirely to send him over a hill's rise and watch him sink out of sight toward sheep that are not in view. When your little dog disappears, it feels so sudden; first you follow his black-and-white body as it arcs through the green, becoming smaller and smaller as he runs. Then poof, abracadabra, there's nothing there but grass and sky.

It takes determination to stay quiet in the emptiness that remains, to stare at the rolling hills and spiky grass with nothing but the jazz riffs of a bluebird to accompany you in your sudden sense of isolation. But willpower is not enough to keep you waiting alone in the emptiness. It takes faith that your dog will do his work without you beside him. It takes forgiveness if you haven't yet brought him up to the task.

And so you wait, forcing yourself to stay still, to let what happens happen, eyes straining for the sign that the sheep have been found and are gathered together, moving back toward you in a semblance of order. You stand and you wait, feet shifting, eyes focused on the point where you think they should appear.

Finally, much later than you think it should be, you see the top of a woolly head, and then a nose, rising up from behind the curve of the hill. And then you see them all, the leader's ears flicking forward and back, chin up, eyes wide and alert. Behind them is your little dog, steady and true, focused on nothing but bringing you the flock, easing them toward you carefully, lest they panic and dart for the woods. Closer and closer they come, and now they are closer still, right beside you, their eyes deep and round, so close that you can almost touch them.

# ACKNOWLEDGMENTS

Acknowledgments can be hard to write. Whom to include, whom to leave out, where to start? But in this case, my job is easy. There is only one place to start—by expressing my gratitude to Jennifer Gates, my literary agent at Zachary, Shuster and Harmsworth. I wrote an entire book, and yet I don't have the words to thank her for all she has done for me. Unless you are lucky enough to have one, you might not know that a great literary agent is an editor, adviser, cheerleader, therapist, and friend. This book would never have been written without Jennifer's encouragement and coaching, and I guarantee that whatever good it contains, much of it is due to her compassionate guidance.

Thanks are also due to everyone at the agency Zachary, Shuster and Harmsworth who has been there for me since long before my first book, *The Other End of the Leash*, came out. A special heartfelt thank-you goes to Esmund Harmsworth, who, first off, is as charming as his name, and whose feedback about earlier drafts of this book was essential in its eventual restructuring. I am ridiculously lucky to have Jen and Esmund in my pack of friends and advisers, as well as all the skilled and hardworking

ACKNOWLEDGMENTS

...eople at Zachary, Shuster and Harmsworth, including Lane Zachary, Todd Shuster, and Chelse Heller.

Speaking of lucky: What a lucky woman I am to have had Leslie Meredith as my editor at Atria. Leslie was the editor for *The Other End of the Leash* and went above and beyond in her efforts to turn a well-intentioned but somewhat sloppy manuscript into a solid book. She taught me as much about writing as anyone ever has, and I was thrilled when Leslie and Atria asked to publish the book you are now reading. Along with being a devoted dog lover (kisses to her corgis), Leslie is the editor every author wants and needs but rarely gets. Lucky me. I am grateful to all at Atria for their efforts and support, including Melanie Iglesias Perez for her reliable assistance, publisher Judith Curr for her belief in the book, and Peter Borland, Paul Olsewski, Yona Deshommes, Jackie Jou, Benjamin Holmes, and Albert Tang.

Sincere appreciation also goes to another Leslie—Leslie Wells, whose editorial guidance saved me when I was floundering with a manuscript that readers loved but that mired them in the murky waters of the Great Memoir Swamp. Her advice and encouragement ("Less is more, unless it's about your mother") was instrumental in refining and improving the manuscript. I hear her voice often now when I'm writing, and if I ever do become the writer I would like to be, the Leslies in my life will deserve much of the credit.

It takes a village to write a good book, and I am amazed at the generosity of friends and colleagues who took the time to read and comment on earlier drafts. Meg and Randy Boscov stand out as especially dedicated readers, and I can't thank them enough for their insightful advice. David Wroblewski (*The Story of Edgar Sawtelle*) took it upon himself, with a generosity that stuns me, to critically evaluate two early drafts, and to teach me everything he could about writing in a couple of months. I learned more from him than I can say, and I hope my efforts here reflect at least some of his skill and generosity. Author Cat Warren (*What the Dog Knows*) carefully read earlier drafts and made excellent suggestions on formatting and structure. I am indebted to her for her insightful suggestions and our continuing cyber- and canine-related friendship.

I am grateful also to Gail Caldwell (*Let's Take the Long Way Home*), who give me essential feedback on an earlier draft, and whose exquisite writing has inspired me ever since I sat transfixed by her first memoir, *A Strong West Wind*. It is the bravery of writers like her, as well as Cheryl Strayed (*Wild, Tiny Beautiful Things*) and Brené Brown (*Daring Greatly, Rising Strong*), who gave me the courage to stop being afraid of being afraid. I am especially lucky to have a real writer in the family, Wendy B. Barker (*One Blackbird at a Time, Nothing Between Us*), whose support and feedback are always like a rain shower in a drought. I drink them up, full of gratitude.

Speaking of sisters, I count myself lucky to have two wonderful ones: Wendy Barker and Liza Piatt (another author, with her own beautiful memoir titled *Dying to Live*), each of whom has provided support and encouragement behind measure. The fact that we have each been simultaneously working on some version of a memoir in the past years says a lot about our family's— especially our father's—love of literature and the written word. My mother, Pamela Dodwell Bean, wasn't as much a reader, but she was a lover of dogs and passionate about curiosity, adventure, and beautiful things, in that order. She supported my love of animals in every way she could, and I will always be grateful to her.

I thank my family for their loving support over the years. I am lucky to be the proud aunt of three amazing nieces—Wendy Piatt, Annie Piatt, and Emily Edwards—along with an equally amazing nephew, David Barker. My husband's family has taken me in as one of their own, and I thank Zach and Sarah, Shane and Rachel, Doug, Roger and Kerry, and mother-in-law Maisie Billings from the bottom of my heart. Grandchildren Taylor and Quinne melt my bones every time I see them, which is never enough.

I also want to thank Julie Hecht (dogspies.com) for her friendship, support, and assistance with research. Along with being brilliant, funny, and inspiring, Julie is my "academic daughter" and makes me happy every time we talk. Lisa Lutz, detective extraordinaire, moved heaven and earth to find the facts behind "the man who fell," and I will always be grateful to her. I am also in debt to the staff at McConnell Publishing, whose dedication, smarts, and hard work have allowed me the time to work on this memoir. Denise Swedlund kept the office functioning like silk for twenty-five years; Lisa Lemberger was and is instrumental in helping me run a business while making time to write. Katie Martz works with me to keep my official Facebook page flowing, which I appreciate every single day of the week. Karen London was the friend and colleague who showed up at my door with flowers when I was at my lowest, and I will always be grateful for that and for our continuing friendship. My friendship with other Certified Applied Animal Behaviorists, including Peter Borchelt, Crista Coppola, Daniel Estep, Suzanne Hetts, Ellen Lindell, Alice Moon-Fanelli, Pamela Reid, Victoria Voith, Camille Ward, John Wright, and Stephen Zawistowski, has been and will continue to be essential to my personal and professional growth. You're my village, and I couldn't have made it this far without you.

My academic mentors, Jeffrey Baylis, Charles Snowdon, and Tony Stretton, have forgotten more than I'll ever know about animal behavior, and I owe them the moon for all that they have taught me, and for the support that they have provided over the years. Lon Hodge (*In Dogs We Trust*) and his noble therapy dog, Gander, have been instrumental in helping me understand the importance of dogs in the recovery of veterans suffering from PTSD.

How can I thank therapists Anne Simon Wolf and Mare Chapman? Working with them was like putting on glasses when you knew the world looked fuzzy but didn't know why. I doubt I ever would have found my voice without them. I wish everyone, no matter what they're dealing with, had the opportunity to learn and grow from their insight, warmth, and skill. Yoga master Scott Anderson also played an important role in my recovery; I introduce him as the man who knows more about the body than anyone else in the world, and I suspect that I am not exaggerating. His combination of knowledge and compassion deserves to be known nationwide. Sarah Watts, my massage therapist for almost two decades, also deserves my sincere thanks for her magical hands, which healed my body and my spirit every time I saw her. I imagine that without Anne, Mare, Scott, and Sarah, I'd be curled up in a corner somewhere, licking my paws like a stressed-out dog.

I owe a great debt to several people whom I have never met. Nancy Venable Raine's book, *After Silence*, did as much as any one thing to help me face the aftermath of being raped. I am deeply thankful for her courage and honesty. Judith Herman's *Trauma and Recovery* also played a significant role in my understanding of all that had happened to me, and was an important part of my recovery.

My two ex-husbands also deserve thanks. You've read about my first husband, Doug McConnell, who taught me so much about enjoying life to the fullest. You haven't read about Patrick Mommaerts, my second husband, and I hereby apologize to him for essentially leaving him out of this story. There were just too many narrative threads to include him, but he was an important part of my life for almost two decades, and I am grateful to him for all that he has given me. Both men are lovely people, and as always, I wish them nothing but happiness.

What would a writer do without friends? Much of writing might be a solitary occupation, but without friends, I can't imagine turning on the computer every morning. I am deeply grateful to friends Peg and Jim Anderson, Rick Axsom, Meg and Randy Boscov, Julie Cullman, David Egger, Donna Huntington, Harriet Irwin, Renee Revetta, Fredericka Schilling, Bonita Sitter, and Sandie Stanfield. They have been as important as food and water to me over the years, and I count myself a lucky woman to have them. And to the person, whomever you are, whom I remember to thank only after it's too late to add your name: Thank you, and I'm sorry.

Another set of friends is equally dear to my heart, and their friendship and wisdom sustain me and my love for working sheepdogs. I offer my thanks to all my friends who compete in sheepdog trials, and to the good people of the Wisconsin Working Sheepdog Association, who work tirelessly to keep border collies true to their heritage. We all remind people, every time we can, that border collies are not happy unless they have a job to do and ample opportunities to use their brains in the way that they were intended

I cannot possibly omit thanking all the clients and dogs I have worked with over the years. They have taught me so much. They filled my life up with joy and heartbreak, peace and drama, for over two decades. All of them were an integral part of my life for so long that I simply wouldn't be who I am today without them. To each of you, a loving hug or a thankful belly rub, depending on the species. I hope that the stories in this book will help others with dogs who behave as if they were traumatized, and emphasize that knowledge and compassion are necessary to help dogs whose behavior is problematic. It's a rare dog who is aggressive because it's fun—these dogs need empathy, not owners who try to impress them with their "dominance."

And Willie? My Willie. My Silly-Billie-Willie-boy. Sometimes it breaks my heart that I can't tell him in words how much I love him, but perhaps it's better this way. All words, no matter how informative, have weight. Surely one of reasons that we love dogs so much is because our relationship is not burdened by the constraints of language. I tell Willie every day how much I love him in every way I can—with the tone of my voice, the touch of my hand, and the attention I pay to his needs. But I can never explain to him that it was his problem behavior that forced me to face what I'd been repressing for so many years. To say that I am grateful to him is inadequate, but I hope this book makes it clear how much I feel that I owe him.

If you have a dog like Willie, with serious behavioral problems, please don't think of them as "dominance" issues. Dogs like Willie need help, not intimidation. You can find resources for troubled dogs at www.TheEducationofWill.com.

Just as these acknowledgments had to begin with Jennifer Gates, they can end only with my gratitude to James Billings, whose love and support are the best things that ever happened to me. I could never have written this book without him. Willie and I both adore him, and rightly so. He is loving and smart and kind and patient and makes me laugh and makes Willie jump for joy when he returns home, and if I were a dog, I would, too. I owe Jim the world, but all I can give him is this little book, along with my eternal gratitude.

# About the Author

Patricia McConnell, PhD, CAAB, is an ethologist and Certified Applied Animal Behaviorist who has consulted with pet owners for over twenty years about serious behavioral problems, specializing in canine aggression. She taught "The Biology and Philosophy of Human/Animal Relationships" in the Department of Zoology at the University of Wisconsin–Madison for twenty-five years and speaks around the world about canine behavior and training. Dr. McConnell is the author of eleven books on training and behavioral problems, as well as the critically acclaimed books *The Other End of the Leash* (translated into fourteen languages), *For the Love of a Dog*, and *Tales of Two Species*. Patricia and her husband live with their working border collies, Willie and Maggie, and their King Charles Cavalier spaniel, Tootsie, outside of Madison, Wisconsin, along with a very spoiled flock of sheep. For more information, go to www.TheEducationofWill.com, www.PatriciaMcConnell.com, or visit her blog at www.TheOtherEndoftheLeash.com.